READING EXPERT

A 5-LEVEL READING COURSE for EFL Readers

4

KB013909

READING EXPERT *4*

Series Editor	Yoo-seung Shin
Project Editors	Mina Song, Hyobin Park, Yuna Kim
Writers	Patrick Ferraro, Elizabeth Young, Keeran Murphy, Nathaniel Galletta, Bryce Olk
Design	Hyunah Song
Editorial Designer	In-sun Lee
Special Thanks to	Seung-pyo Han, Hoe-young Kim, Hey-won Nam

Copyright©2020 by NE Neungyule, Inc.

First Printing 5 January 2020

12th Printing 15 August 2024

All rights reserved. No part of this publication may be reproduced, stored in a retrieval system, or transmitted in any form or by any means, electronic, mechanical, photocopying, recording, or otherwise, without the prior permission of the publisher.

ISBN   979-11-253-2930-5

Photo Credits

www.istockphoto.com

www.shutterstock.com

www.dreamstime.com

INTRODUCTION

R eading Expert is a five-level reading course for EFL readers, with special relevance for junior and senior high school students. They will acquire not only reading skills but also knowledge of various contemporary and academic topics.

FEATURES

Covering Current, Academic Topics: Topics ranging from real world issues to academic subjects are covered in an easy and interesting way so that junior and senior high school students can understand them. These subjects appeal to students and can hold their attention.

Expanding Knowledge: Each unit is composed of two articles under one topic heading. These articles will help students expand their knowledge of various topics, including social and academic issues.

Practicing Reading Skills: Reading comprehension checkups encourage the use of important reading skills. They can be used to evaluate and improve students' comprehension skills, such as identifying main ideas, specific details, and implied meanings.

Tackling Longer Passages: EFL junior and senior high school students often find it difficult to read long passages because they have not received much exposure to lengthy material. Interesting and well-developed passages customized for EFL students will help learners to approach longer passages with ease. Summarizing exercises will also help them understand the flow of long passages.

Test-Oriented Questions: Many comprehension checkup questions are similar to TOEFL questions. They will be a stepping stone in preparing students for English tests at school, as well as for official English language tests such as TOEFL.

LEVEL	GRADE	WORDS LIMITS	UNITS
Reading Expert 1	Low-Intermediate	230 - 270	15
Reading Expert 2	Intermediate	250 - 300	15
Reading Expert 3		270 - 330	15
Reading Expert 4	Low-Advanced	**290 - 350**	**15**
Reading Expert 5		300 - 370	15

TO THE **STUDENTS**

Why Is Reading Challenging?

It is a very challenging, sometimes painful, experience for EFL students to read English newspapers, magazines, or books. There are various reasons for this: the high level of vocabulary and sentence structure, a lack of background knowledge on the topic, and a need for certain reading skills.

Become an Expert Reader with Reading Expert!

Reading Expert is a five-level reading course that is intended to improve your reading abilities gradually. There are 4 areas of reading strategies you need to focus on to improve your reading abilities.

1. Vocabulary Skills

When you run into an unfamiliar word, try to continue reading. In many cases a couple of unfamiliar words will not prevent general understanding of a passage. If you think they are still a barrier to further reading, use context clues. If they also do not provide enough information, it will be necessary to use your Word Book or look up the "problem word" in a dictionary.

2. Paragraph Approach

A passage is a collection of paragraphs, and the main point of each paragraph is organized into the main idea of the passage. When you read a passage, try not to just focus on the meaning of each sentence: Keep asking yourself, "What is the main point of this paragraph?" Questions on the main point of a paragraph and summary exercises will help you stay focused.

3. Understanding Long Passages

Young EFL readers have often not been exposed to long passages (more than 200 words), and they may find such passages difficult to understand. Various reading skills will be needed to understand long passages: scanning, skimming, understanding the structure of the passage, etc. Reading comprehension questions and summary exercises cover these reading skills.

4. Knowledge of the Topic

Just like when you're reading in your native language, a lack of background knowledge can prevent you from understanding the topic. The Reading Expert course covers a variety of topics, including academic subjects, social issues, world culture, and more. If you are not familiar with the topic in question, try to search for relevant information in books or on the Internet.

TO THE **TEACHER**

Series Overview

Reading Expert is a five-level reading course written by EFL teachers who have years of experience in teaching EFL students. It is simple to use in a classroom and interesting enough to keep students' attention. Each level is composed of 15 units, and each unit has two readings. Each unit contains the following sections:

Before Reading

The WARM-UP QUESTION before each reading is intended to get students ready by relating the topic to their lives. You can also help students by introducing background knowledge or explaining difficult words.

Readings

There are two readings for every unit. Before having students read the text, explain to them some important reading skills, such as scanning and skimming. After reading the passage, they can listen to an MP3 audio recording. Each reading is followed by a WORD CHECK. Students can use this section to practice guessing the meanings of the key words and expressions in context. WORD FOCUS, which shows collocations, synonyms, and antonyms, is provided alongside the passages. It will familiarize students with some natural English expressions while increasing their range of English vocabulary.

Comprehension Checkups

Readings are also followed by comprehension checkup questions. These are intended to help students identify the MAIN IDEA or subject of the passage and understand DETAILS. Questions related to reading skills are sometimes included.

Summary

A SUMMARY is provided for each reading and it can take a number of different forms, such as a basic summary, a graphic organizer, a note-taking summary, etc. All of these forms are designed to improve students' ability to understand and summarize a passage. There are various ways to use this section, such as assigning it as homework or having the students complete it without referring to the reading. It tests whether students understand the text as a whole.

Word Review Test

Learning vocabulary is important for EFL readers. They need to review key words, expressions, and difficult or unfamiliar words. A WORD REVIEW TEST comes at the end of every two units and is intended to test students' vocabulary.

TABLE OF **CONTENTS**

Welcome to Ecuador

WARM-UP QUESTION • Can you name the countries that the equator runs through?

Here is an interesting fact: Despite circling the entire globe, the equator runs through just 13 countries. One of these nations takes its name from the Spanish word for equator: the Republic of Ecuador.

Ecuador is located on the northwest coast of South America,
5 sandwiched between Colombia to the north and Peru to the south. In 1736, a French mathematician named Charles-Marie de La Condamine traveled to the area that is now Ecuador and conducted a series of measurements. His work showed that our planet, once considered to be a perfect sphere, is actually flatter at the poles and bulges at the equator.

10 Today, La Condamine's work is remembered with a 30-meter-tall tower in a park named Mitad del Mundo, which means "middle of the world." The park even has a yellow line running through it, which is said to mark the location of the equator.

_____(A)_____, GPS technology shows that the actual equator is located 240 meters to the north. Despite this, thousands of visitors each year photograph one
15 another standing with one foot on either side of the line. They don't care whether the line is accurate or not—they just want a fun memory of their trip to the equator.

For those interested in geographical accuracy, a visit to the Intiñan Solar Museum is recommended. Just a two-minute drive from Mitad del Mundo, the museum claims that GPS calculations have proved it to be located exactly at 0 degrees latitude. At
20 the museum, guides demonstrate special scientific "experiments."

_____(B)_____, a sink is placed right on the equator to show that water goes straight down the drain. It doesn't spin to the left or right as it is supposed to! And visitors are encouraged to try to balance an egg on top of a nail. The guides claim this is only possible at the
25 equator. Although these experiments are not scientifically true, they are still a lot of fun!

With or without scientific facts, a visit to the equator is a memorable experience. Besides being a fun place to take photos, the equator reminds us that we live on a big, (almost) round planet
30 traveling through space!

WORD CHECK

Choose the correct words for the blanks from the highlighted words in the passage.

1. _____ a three-dimensional figure that is completely round
2. _____ including all the parts of sth
3. _____ worth remembering
4. _____ to keep sth from falling or leaning one way
5. _____ to explain sth by actually doing it

*sb: somebody / sth: something

1 What is the best title for the passage?

    a. An Exploration of the Equator in Ecuador

    b. The Development of GPS Technology in Ecuador

    c. Nations That the Equator Runs Through

    d. The Importance of Geographical Accuracy

DETAILS

2 What did La Condamine's work show according to paragraph 2?

_____

3 What is the best pair for blanks (A) and (B)?

	(A)	(B)
a.	In contrast	Furthermore
b.	Therefore	For instance
c.	On the one hand	In addition
d.	However	For example

4 What does the underlined part in paragraph 4 mean?

    a. Water in a sink always drains straight down.

    b. Water going down a drain is expected to turn to the left or right.

    c. Water on the equator flows faster than in any other place.

    d. Water on the equator is believed to turn to the left or right.

5 Which of the following is NOT true according to the passage?

    a. Ecuador's name comes from the Spanish word for equator.

    b. Mitad del Mundo means "middle of the world."

    c. According to GPS, the yellow line in the park marks the actual equator.

    d. In the Intiñan Solar Museum, visitors can enjoy interesting experiments.

SUMMARY

6 Use the words in the box to fill in the blanks.

equator	latitude	conduct	measurements	explore	mark	sphere

Ecuador is one of 13 countries crossed by the _____. It gets its name from a Spanish word. In 1736, a French mathematician took scientific _____ there and found out that our planet is not a perfect _____. Today, his work is memorialized with a tower in a park called Mitad del Mundo. There is a yellow line running through the park that is said to _____ the equator. However, GPS shows the equator to be 240 meters to the north. Near the park, you can find the Intiñan Solar Museum, where guides _____ fun experiments.

Seven kilometers from the coast of Cape Town, South Africa, is a UNESCO world heritage site called Robben Island. When the Dutch came to settle in South Africa in 1652, the largest animals living on the island were seals. In fact, the name "Robben" is 5 derived from the Dutch word meaning "seal." What makes this island valuable, however, is its history during the colonial period.

As more colonists moved into Africa, conflicts with the people already living there sprang up everywhere. Therefore, the Dutch needed a place to imprison whoever fought 10 against them, and they chose Robben Island. Soldiers, civilians, and leaders of various tribes were imprisoned on the island. Even kings and princes who defied Dutch rule in faraway colonies were brought there to be prisoners.

During the 1800s, Robben Island became a prison for people with serious illnesses as well. People who were mentally ill or had leprosy were sent to the island to keep them 15 far from others. At first, some of them were allowed to leave if they wanted, but later they were forced to stay. This practice remained in place until 1931.

Under the government-approved system of racial discrimination known as apartheid, Robben Island was used as a maximum security prison for political leaders who wanted racial equality. The most famous of these was Nelson Mandela, who was 20 imprisoned there for 18 years, from 1964 to 1982. Nelson Mandela's imprisonment drew international attention to South Africa, which increased the pressure to end apartheid. Robben Island's time as a prison ended in 1991 due to South Africans' efforts to undo apartheid policies. Because of Mandela and others who faced **hardship** for the cause of equality, Robben Island became a symbol of _____ (A) _____ .

25 In 1997, the many historical sites on Robben Island were turned into a museum. Since then, the Robben Island Museum has run school programs and tours to educate people about the island's history. By remembering the injustice of the past, people can be motivated to create a better future.

WORD FOCUS

⊜ Synonyms for

hardship

difficulty
adversity
suffering
misfortune

WORD CHECK

Choose the correct words for the blanks from the highlighted words in the passage.

1. _____ distant from a particular place or most places
2. _____ relating to more than one nation
3. _____ anyone who isn't a member of the military or the police
4. _____ a situation in which all people have the same status, rights, and opportunities
5. _____ a serious disagreement between people, groups, or countries

1   What is the best title for the passage?
    a. The Island of Suffering and Triumph
    b. Nelson Mandela and a New South Africa
    c. Robben Island: The First Prison in the World
    d. Untold Stories Behind Dutch Colonization

2   Which is NOT mentioned about Robben Island?
    a. where it is located
    b. when it became a UNESCO world heritage site
    c. what its name comes from
    d. what purpose the Dutch used it for

3   What effect did Nelson Mandela's imprisonment have on South Africa?
    _____

4   What is the best expression for blank (A)?
    a. power and authority   b. overcoming oppression
    c. protest against war   d. the struggle for survival

5   Write T if the statement is true or F if it's false.
    (1) Dutch colonists used Robben Island as a vacation spot.   _____
    (2) Patients with leprosy weren't allowed to stay on Robben Island.   _____
    (3) In modern times, Robben Island has been used for educational purposes.   _____

6   Match each topic to the correct paragraph in the passage.
    (1) Paragraph 1 •   • ⓐ the forced isolation of sick people
    (2) Paragraph 2 •   • ⓑ the imprisonment of rebels from Dutch colonies
    (3) Paragraph 3 •   • ⓒ the location of Robben Island and the meaning of its
                                     name
    (4) Paragraph 4 •   • ⓓ Robben Island as an educational site
    (5) Paragraph 5 •   • ⓔ the holding of political prisoners in recent history

Water Sommelier

When you hear the word "sommelier," you probably think of wine. Traditionally, sommeliers are experts in wine who help diners choose an appropriate wine to go with their meal. But there is also another kind of
5 sommelier—one who is an expert in water.

Water sommeliers can detect the smallest differences in how different types of water taste. On a daily basis, you probably don't think about the taste of water, but if
10 you travel to a new place, you might notice that the water tastes different than the water you are used to. That's because the water we drink contains all kinds of different salts and minerals that give it a unique
15 taste. For this reason, some high-class restaurants offer water selections for their diners to choose from. A water sommelier helps the restaurant build this list and also recommends which kind of water will pair
20 best with which dishes.

So how do water sommeliers taste water? First, they raise the glass to their nose and breathe in deeply to enjoy any faint aromas. Next, they take a smaller sip, move the water around their tongue, and swallow it. 25 This process allows the sommelier to detect all of the water's delicate flavors. Particular words are used to describe the taste of the water, such as "acidity," "effervescence," and "structure." Respectively, these refer 30 to the water's freshness, its bubbles, and how rich and complex its taste is.

Restaurants are focusing more and more on the water that they serve. One restaurant in Los Angeles, for example, 35 offers a selection of 20 different kinds of water from all over the world. Their most expensive water costs 20 dollars per bottle! So next time you take a drink of water, don't just swallow it. Take a moment to think about 40 how it tastes!

WORD CHECK

Choose the correct words for the blanks from the highlighted words in the passage.

1. _____ separately and in the mentioned order
2. _____ certain or specific
3. _____ one who is highly skilled in a particular industry or subject
4. _____ to take air into the lungs, especially through the mouth or nose
5. _____ having qualities that are fine or subtle

READING SKILL

Skimming
Skimming involves looking quickly through the text to get a general idea of what it is about. We move our eyes quickly through the whole text, allowing us to identify the purpose of the passage or the main idea.

MAIN IDEA

1 **What is the passage mainly about?**
   a. what water sommeliers do
   b. ways to become a professional sommelier
   c. what makes water taste unique
   d. the contrast between wine sommeliers and water sommeliers

DETAILS

2 **Why does the water we drink have different tastes?**

_____

3 **Which is NOT mentioned as a task of a water sommelier?**
   a. detecting water's subtly different flavors
   b. making a water list on a menu
   c. suggesting water that goes with certain foods
   d. investigating customers' water preferences

4 **Put the following information about how water sommeliers taste water in order.**

| _____ → _____ → _____ → ⓓ |

   ⓐ moving water around the tongue   ⓑ taking in water's aromas
   ⓒ sipping water   ⓓ swallowing water

5 **Which is the closest in meaning to <u>selection</u>?**
   a. introduction   b. procedure   c. range   d. competition

SUMMARY

6 Use the words in the box to fill in the blanks.

| matches   thinks   aroma   diners   taste   detects   sommeliers |

Water contains salts and minerals that give it a unique taste. These days, many restaurants want to offer their _____ a wide selection of waters to choose from. A water sommelier is a person who helps restaurants create a water list and decides which water _____ best with which dish. The sommelier _____ water's delicate flavors by smelling its _____ and moving it around his or her tongue. The taste of the water is described using certain words. Nowadays, restaurants are paying more attention to the water that they serve.

WARM-UP QUESTION • What kind of job would you like in the near future?

We live in a rapidly changing world. And as our world changes, so do our jobs. There are many issues that are currently affecting the job market. They include efforts to reduce environmental damage, the aging of populations, and the rapid advancement of technology. With these in mind, here are some jobs that haven't been created yet but probably will be soon.

You may have heard of website designers and fashion designers, but what about garbage designers? Although this job title might sound strange, the primary task of garbage designers is to find new uses for old products that would otherwise be thrown away. This process, known as upcycling, helps reduce the amount of trash sent to landfills. Some garbage designers also modify manufacturing processes to reduce the amount of waste produced by factories. Over time, they may completely redesign the way companies make things!

Nostalgists are another new kind of designer. They design special homes for wealthy senior citizens who would like to be reminded of the happiest times of their lives. Rather than living in a typical modern apartment, they can have a living space that looks like a home from the 1970s or 80s. People are living longer lives these days, and the populations of many countries are aging rapidly. Nostalgists, along with many other specialists, will aim to meet the needs of this growing age group.

Robots are expected to eliminate jobs rather than create them. But robot counselors are an exception! Soon there will be robots that can drive cars, cook meals, and clean homes. The role of robot counselors will be to meet with families and assist them in choosing the robots that best fit their needs. They will also help **family** members adjust to having robots in their lives by providing ongoing customer service. If a robot doesn't work out, they can work with families to pick a new one.

Of course, no one knows exactly what the future holds. But it is highly likely that some of today's familiar jobs will disappear and be replaced by new and unusual occupations.

WORD FOCUS

🔄 Collocations for

family

family **ties**
family **business**
nuclear *family*
extended *family*

WORD CHECK

Choose the correct words for the blanks from the highlighted words in the passage.

1. _____ to try to fulfill or meet a goal
2. _____ to remove or take away completely
3. _____ state of improving and developing sth
4. _____ to make a small change as an improvement
5. _____ the first or most important

1 What is the passage mainly about?

    a. jobs that are disappearing

    b. interesting occupations unknown to most people

    c. jobs that do not exist but will be created soon

    d. new jobs that come from advances in technology

DETAILS

2 What is the primary task of garbage designers?

_____

3 Which is closest in meaning to typical?

    a. recent   b. popular   c. normal   d. strange

4 Which is NOT mentioned as a task of robot counselors?

    a. programming robots to do chores

    b. recommending the proper robots for families

    c. aiding families in becoming accustomed to new robots

    d. choosing another robot when families are not satisfied

5 Which of the following is NOT true according to the passage?

    a. Pollution, an aging society, and technology are influencing the job market.

    b. Garbage designers change the manufacturing methods of factories to decrease waste.

    c. Nostalgists create homes for seniors that are inspired by past decades.

    d. Robots are expected to create many jobs in the near future instead of removing them.

SUMMARY

6 Use the words in the box to fill in the blanks.

reduce	common	new	dumping	adjusting	seniors	population

Future Jobs

Garbage Designer	▪ finds _____ ways to use old products ▪ redesigns factory processes to _____ waste
Nostalgist	▪ designs special homes for _____ ▪ makes their residences resemble their best years from the past
Robot Counselor	▪ assists families trying to choose the proper household robot ▪ provides customer service to people having trouble _____ to their robots

WORD REVIEW TEST

[1~3] Choose the word that is closest in meaning to the underlined word.

1. The boy claimed that he saw a UFO.
    a. denied   b. required   c. concealed   d. insisted

2. The doctor needs accurate information in order to provide effective treatment.
    a. precise   b. improper   c. outdated   d. intimate

3. Passengers are not allowed to use any mobile devices after take-off.
    a. created   b. informed   c. permitted   d. punished

[4~6] Connect the matching words in columns A and B.

A	B
4. draw •	• a. the best tourist attraction
5. fight against •	• b. public attention
6. recommend •	• c. injustice

[7~10] Choose the best word to complete each sentence.

7. Police officers _____ an investigation of the crime scene.
    a. forced   b. placed   c. conducted   d. imprisoned

8. The result _____ that their theory can be applied to every age group.
    a. proved   b. settled   c. educated   d. motivated

9. He _____ his illness and became the player of the year.
    a. increased   b. overcame   c. marked   d. located

10. The city _____ a language school for children during summer vacation.
    a. circles   b. remembers   c. runs   d. balances

[11~12] Circle the odd one out in each group.

11. memory   retention   recollection   intelligence

12. location   aisle   position   site

[13~15] Choose the correct word for each definition.

symbol defy undo practice equator remind

13. to make someone remember or think about something:

14. to refuse to obey a rule or law:

15. the usual way of doing something as a result of social custom:

[1~4] Choose the word that is closest in meaning to the underlined word.

1. Some occupations require people to wear uniforms.
   a. degrees   b. aims   c. operations   d. jobs

2. I don't think jeans are appropriate for the party.
   a. fancy   b. proper   c. casual   d. odd

3. You should have regular checkups to detect diseases such as cancer.
   a. find   b. remove   c. treat   d. affect

4. The chef served us a delicious dinner.
   a. achieved   b. provided   c. performed   d. bought

[5~8] Connect the matching words in columns A and B.

A		B
5. design •		• a. environmental damage
6. meet •		• b. special houses
7. contain •		• c. the needs of people
8. reduce •		• d. salts and minerals

[9~12] Choose the best word to complete each sentence. (Change the form if needed.)

disappear particular manufacture familiar complex cost

9. The tickets to the concert _____ 10 dollars each.

10. Her face looks _____, but I don't remember her name.

11. Humpback whales are quickly _____ because of hunting.

12. The layout of the building is so _____ that it is hard to find the emergency stairs.

[13~16] Choose the correct word for each definition.

currently swallow faint unusual selection population

13. difficult to detect due to being weak:

14. now; at the present time:

15. all the people residing in a specific region:

16. to move something from your mouth to your stomach:

Teaching English

WARM-UP QUESTION • Do you think you have to speak English just like a native speaker?

I'm Eric Smith, and I've been teaching English to non-native speakers for nearly 20 years. One common problem I've seen is students not speaking because they're afraid of making a mistake. Whenever I see a student "handcuffed" by his or her inability to speak Standard English, I ask

5 myself, "Is speaking Standard English really that important?"

These days, English functions as a tool for global communication. Traveling through airports, I'm always struck by how many conversations between strangers are taking place in English, even though it's not the first language of either of the speakers. A Korean airline worker might be

10 answering the questions of a French passenger in English. Or a Vietnamese man might be using English to discuss the local food with a woman from Egypt. As a native speaker, I sometimes have a hard time figuring out what they're talking about, but they usually seem to understand each other just fine.

15 More interestingly, English is being changed in some countries. People in different countries modify it to make it fit their native culture. In Malaysia, for example, people speak a dialect they call Manglish, which is English combined with bits of Chinese and Malay. In particular, the word "lah" is often used. Its usage is varied, but it can be used to change a verb into an imperative. For instance, the verb "drink" in English can be

20 made a command by saying "Drink, lah!"

All of the examples above are evidence of how English is being used practically. Don't get me wrong: I still think it's very important for students to learn how to read and write Standard English. But it's also important to understand that there is more than one way to speak the language, especially when your main desire is to communicate.

25 Students who learn to switch back and forth between Standard English and practical English will be best prepared to succeed in our global future.

WORD CHECK

Choose the correct words for the blanks from the highlighted words in the passage.

1. _____ belonging to a particular area
2. _____ a regional form of a language
3. _____ to serve a certain purpose
4. _____ to change from one thing to another
5. _____ including many different types

READING SKILL

Separating facts and opinions
We tend to accept the information we read as truth, which is not desirable. When we read, we need to confirm whether the writer is using facts or opinions. Facts can be proven while opinions contain the writer's personal beliefs.

MAIN IDEA

1 **What is the passage mainly about?**

   a. teaching English to non-native speakers
   b. the functional usage of English
   c. the necessity of Standard English
   d. preparing for a global future

DETAILS

2 **What does the underlined part in paragraph 1 mean?**

   a. being afraid of making mistakes when speaking English
   b. being able to speak correct Standard English
   c. being unable to speak English with people from other countries
   d. being satisfied with his or her own use of Standard English

3 **Who has the same perspective as Eric Smith regarding English?**

> James: To learn a language, we should first learn its rules.
> Ann: Language is just a tool for exchanging thoughts.
> Sean: Accuracy is important when communicating with each other.
> Sue: Dialects from different regions and countries should be avoided.

   a. James   b. Ann   c. Sean   d. Sue

4 **Write F if the statement is a fact or O if it is an opinion.**

   (1) English is being changed in some countries.   _____
   (2) "Lah" can be used to make an imperative in Manglish.   _____
   (3) It is important to use Standard English too.   _____
   (4) There is more than one way to speak English.   _____

SUMMARY

5 **Use the words in the box to fill in the blanks.**

> communicate   practical   mistakes   evidence   necessary   modify   dialect

The writer teaches English and thinks many students have trouble speaking English because they worry too much about making _____. But in his opinion, it's not always _____ to speak Standard English. He points out that many people use English to speak with other non-native speakers. He explains how people in some countries, such as Malaysia, have created their own _____ of English. He feels that learning Standard English is important, but it is okay to _____ in "non-Standard English."

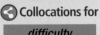
WARM-UP QUESTION • What do you think is the main function of the brain?

Aphasia is a language disorder that makes it very difficult to communicate. It is caused by brain damage, often resulting from a stroke or head injury. Aphasia is classified according to the
5 location of the brain injury, as damage to different parts of the brain causes different problems. Two of the most common types are Broca's and Wernicke's aphasia. The following examples may help you imagine what it is like to suffer from these conditions.

Someone with Broca's aphasia is very likely to come out with a sentence such as
10 "Walk dog." But what does this mean? The dog wants to go for a walk? Let's walk the dog? There are many possible ways to interpret this sentence because there are no pronouns, prepositions, or conjunctions to tell us "who" is doing "what." People with Broca's aphasia have **difficulty** making grammatically correct sentences. For these people, getting others to understand them is difficult and frustrating.

15 _____(A)_____, Wernicke's aphasia causes problems with comprehension. People suffering from this condition can speak easily but have trouble understanding others. This means their conversations often don't make sense. For example, you might ask a person with Wernicke's aphasia, "Did you have lunch?" He or she may respond with something like this: "You know that I want him to visit." As you can imagine, conversations are just
20 as difficult for these people.

Normally, speech therapy is recommended as treatment for aphasia. It helps some patients learn to overcome their difficulties and communicate more effectively with their limited abilities. Aphasia patients also need help from others. Family members can play an important role in aiding aphasia patients with their communication, emotional, and
25 psychological problems.

WORD FOCUS

◀ Collocations for

difficulty

cause *difficulties*
overcome *difficulties*
major *difficulty*
financial *difficulty*

WORD
CHECK

Choose the correct words for the blanks from the highlighted words in the passage.

1. _____ in a way that produces good results
2. _____ damage to a part of the body
3. _____ a mental or physical problem that affects health
4. _____ to answer or reply
5. _____ to explain the meaning of sth

MAIN IDEA

1 What is the passage mainly about?

a. a way to avoid grammatical mistakes
b. different therapies for different language disorders
c. a language disorder that makes communication difficult
d. a way to improve communication skills

DETAILS

2 What problem do people with Broca's aphasia have when forming sentences?

_____

3 What is the best expression for blank (A)?

a. In a similar way   b. In contrast   c. Otherwise   d. In other words

4 What can help aphasia patients according to the passage? [Choose two.]

a. speech therapy   b. learning reading skills
c. family support   d. grammar correction

5 Which is NOT mentioned about aphasia?

a. what it is caused by
b. the difference between Broca's and Wernicke's aphasia
c. possible illnesses resulting from it
d. what kind of treatment is suggested

SUMMARY

6 Use the words in the box to fill in the blanks.

| grammatically emotion respond interpret communication damage effectively |

Aphasia

Definition	a disorder that prevents normal _____
Cause and Effect	▪ caused by _____ to the brain ▪ leads to problems with spoken language
The Most Common Types	▪ Broca's: Patients cannot create sentences that are _____ correct. ▪ Wernicke's: Patients cannot _____ logically to the sentences of others.

WARM-UP QUESTION • Have you ever experienced discrimination because of your age?

Discrimination is the act of treating people unfairly because of a certain characteristic that they possess. You probably know all about racism and sexism, but you may not realize that people can also be treated unfairly due to their age. This is known as ageism.

5 The term "ageism" was first used in 1969 by Robert Butler, an American doctor and author who was interested in protecting the rights of the elderly. He created it to help bring attention to the social problems older people sometimes face.

 Although it is often said that we must respect the elderly, many of us believe 10 the stereotypes that they are slow, have bad memories, or are unable to learn how to use modern technology. The elderly are also sometimes stereotyped as being poor decision-makers who are uncreative and resistant to change. This kind of image can be quite harmful to senior citizens, especially when they are in the workplace or trying to find a new job.

15 However, the elderly aren't the only ones who can experience ageism. Teenagers and young adults sometimes face similar problems. Some companies refuse to hire younger workers, or they pay them a lower wage than older employees. There is also the issue of unpaid internships. Although they are designed to provide work experience, they are sometimes used to take advantage of youthful jobseekers, manipulating them 20 into providing free labor.

 Like the elderly, young people also have to deal with certain negative stereotypes. Some are denied promotions at work because their managers have the opinion that young people are lazy and **unreliable**; others are turned away from apartment buildings because the landlords feel that young people are irresponsible and noisy.

25 These days more and more people are becoming aware of the issues caused by ageism. However, it can be a difficult problem to eliminate. Many of the stereotypes related to age have become an accepted part of society. But we can all do our part by remembering to treat every person like a unique individual, no matter how old or how young they are.

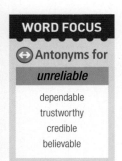

WORD FOCUS

⟳ Antonyms for
unreliable

dependable
trustworthy
credible
believable

WORD CHECK

Choose the correct words for the blanks from the highlighted words in the passage.

1. _____ to have or be the owner of sth
2. _____ to reject sth
3. _____ a fixed idea concerning a type of person
4. _____ opposed to sth
5. _____ the unfair treatment of people based on race

MAIN IDEA

1 **What is the passage mainly about?**

a. the origin of ageism

b. how to deal with prejudice against the elderly

c. problems caused by age discrimination

d. the conflict between the old and the young

DETAILS

2 **Why did Robert Butler make the term "ageism"?**

_____

3 **Which is NOT mentioned as a stereotype of the elderly?**

a. They are poor at remembering things.

b. They are hard to get along with.

c. They have difficulty learning new technology.

d. They are unwilling to embrace change.

4 **Which is closest in meaning to take advantage of?**

a. benefit   b. exploit   c. employ   d. operate

5 **Which of the following is NOT true according to the passage?**

a. The elderly can have a hard time in the workplace because of stereotypes.

b. Older employees are often paid less than younger workers.

c. One stereotype about the young is that they lack responsibility.

d. Ageism can be experienced by both the young and the elderly.

SUMMARY

6 **Use the words in the box to fill in the blanks.**

| rights refuse experience individuals discrimination society employment |

Ageism is a form of _____ based on age. The term was created in 1969 by an American doctor concerned about the _____ of the elderly. Older people often face negative stereotypes which cause them to have difficulties at work or in finding a job. Young people also _____ ageism. Some are denied _____, paid a lower wage, or offered only unpaid internships. They also have to deal with negative stereotypes. The best way to fight ageism is to look at people as _____ regardless of their age.

WARM-UP QUESTION • Did you know that some animals are raised in poor conditions?

The traditional image of a farm is a quiet place in the countryside run by a farmer who takes good care of his or her animals. But in reality, about two thirds of the world's farm animals are currently
5 being raised in factory farms. And these factory farms are very different from our peaceful image of farm life.

Factory farms are large, crowded places that put corporate profits before the health and safety of their animals. These animals are packed together so tightly that they can barely move, often spending their entire lives indoors. In order to make the animals grow
10 faster, factory farms give them growth hormones. This unnatural growth **cause**s many physical problems, including chronic pain and heart issues. When these animals grow too sick, they are not even treated. Instead, they are simply killed to cut costs.

Moreover, factory farms damage the environment and have adverse effects on the health of humans. Keeping so many animals in one place means that a lot of waste is
15 generated. This waste can pollute the air, land, and water of the surrounding community. Factory farms also require large amounts of water and energy to operate. They can be a threat to consumers as well. Bacteria such as *salmonella can thrive in unsanitary conditions, contaminating the meat, milk, and eggs that come from factory farms. Animals are given large doses of antibiotics to combat such bacteria, but this causes
20 a bigger problem. The bacteria simply evolve and become stronger, creating a serious health risk to humans.

So how can we help end the harmful practices of factory farms? First of all, we can start by purchasing only meat and dairy products that come from farms that meet high animal welfare and environmental standards. These products are generally indicated by
25 special labels, such as "Animal Welfare Approved." We can also encourage politicians to pass strict laws banning cruelty to animals. Although it may be impossible to completely eliminate factory farming, efforts such as these will help ensure that farms treat their animals better.

*salmonella: a type of bacteria that can cause food poisoning

WORD FOCUS

◀ **Collocations for**

cause

cause **concern**
cause **chaos**
cause **disease**
cause **damage**

WORD CHECK

Choose the correct words for the blanks from the highlighted words in the passage.

1. _____ right now, at the present moment
2. _____ to grow stronger or be successful
3. _____ long lasting or continual
4. _____ related to a large company
5. _____ harmful or unfavorable

1   What is the best title for the passage?

   a. New Solutions to Farming Problems
   b. The Two Sides of Factory Farming
   c. The Cruel Reality of Factory Farms
   d. The Reasons for Factory Farming

2   Which is NOT true about animals in factory farms according to paragraph 2?

   a. They don't get to go outside often.
   b. They are given hormones so that they can grow faster.
   c. They suffer from health problems because they are injected with hormones.
   d. When they get sick, they are treated with cheap, low-quality medicine.

3   Which is NOT mentioned as a problem caused by factory farming?

   a. The waste from the farms pollutes the surrounding areas.
   b. Lots of energy is used to maintain the farms.
   c. The unclean conditions of the farms contaminate their products.
   d. There are not enough antibiotics to protect the animals from salmonella.

4   What can we encourage politicians to do to help farm animals?

   _____

5   Which is closest in meaning to eliminate?

   a. remove   b. decrease   c. establish   d. exclude

6   Use the words in the box to fill in the blanks.

operate   pollute   profits   standards   labels   antibiotics   waste

Factory Farms

Practices	• value _____ over animal welfare • keep animals in crowded, unsanitary conditions • give animals hormones and large amounts of _____
Problems	• make animals suffer • _____ the environment • cause health risks to people
Responses	• buy food from farms that meet certain _____ • encourage politicians to pass laws protecting animals

WORD REVIEW TEST

[1~3] **Choose the word that is closest in meaning to the underlined word.**

1. UNICEF has taken the responsibility of <u>aiding</u> children in need.
   a. helping   b. funding   c. raising   d. pleasing

2. The student's argument doesn't <u>fit</u> the topic.
   a. reflect   b. suit   c. combine   d. prepare

3. I wasn't able to <u>figure out</u> how to solve this question.
   a. ask   b. respond   c. understand   d. correct

[4~7] **Connect the matching words in columns A and B.**

A	B
4. suffer from	a. a dialect
5. speak	b. a condition
6. answer	c. airports
7. travel through	d. the question

[8~9] **Choose the best word to complete each sentence.**

8. I'm trying to _____ my fear of swimming.
   a. discuss   b. function   c. overcome   d. cause

9. The school offers work experience programs to satisfy _____ interests of students.
   a. varied   b. frustrating   c. emotional   d. native

[10~12] **Circle the odd one out in each group.**

10.	damage	injury	wound	therapy
11.	modify	classify	alter	change
12.	recommend	refuse	deny	turn down

[13~15] **Choose the correct word for each definition.**

comprehension   inability   disorder   command   desire   evidence

13. the act of understanding something:

14. a definitive order to do something:

15. a strong wish to have something:

[1~3] Choose the word that is closest in meaning to the underlined word.

1. He has <u>run</u> a Korean restaurant in the United States.
    a. constructed   b. confirmed   c. maintained   d. operated

2. Climate change is a major <u>threat</u> to our planet.
    a. drawback   b. danger   c. ailment   d. warning

3. One important <u>characteristic</u> of detectives is the power of observation.
    a. shape   b. stereotype   c. trait   d. attention

[4~6] Connect the matching words in columns A and B.

A	B
4. face •	• a. the atmosphere
5. pollute •	• b. cruel activities
6. ban •	• c. a difficult challenge

[7~9] Choose the best word to complete each sentence.

7. The disease spread rapidly due to _____ conditions.
    a. irresponsible   b. noisy   c. unsanitary   d. similar

8. His testimony is _____ because he is biased against the suspect.
    a. uncreative   b. serious   c. chronic   d. unreliable

9. Regular exercise helps the body _____ toxins.
    a. eliminate   b. generate   c. possess   d. require

[10~12] Circle the odd one out in each group.

10. fact   opinion   truth   reality

11. special   peculiar   unique   resistant

12. equality   fairness   justice   discrimination

[13~15] Choose the correct word for each definition.

welfare   manipulate   treat   antibiotics   contaminate   cruelty

13. drugs used to prevent infections:

14. behavior that deliberately hurts others:

15. to control the actions of others in a devious way:

UNIT

05

History

READING 1

WORD FOCUS

⊜ Synonyms for

separation

division
disunion
split-up

WORD CHECK

WARM-UP QUESTION • Have you learned about Ireland's history?

D id you know that the island of Ireland and the country of Ireland are not the same? Part of the island is designated as Northern Ireland and belongs to the United Kingdom. In fact, for 120 years, the entire island was under the UK's rule. How did this happen, and how did Ireland become its own country?

Ever since several invasions in the 1100s, England had some political influence over Ireland. At first both countries were Catholic, but in the 1500s, King Henry VIII of England adopted Protestantism as the state religion, which applied to Ireland, as well. Unhappy with the change, the Irish leaders rebelled against England. English rulers restricted the political and economic activities of any Irish who refused to convert to Protestantism. Furthermore, they encouraged Protestants to move to Ireland and gave them land confiscated from Irish owners.

In 1800, the English introduced a bill that would remove restrictions that prohibited Catholics from holding political office if Ireland agreed to join the UK. Although the act became official on January 1, 1801, discrimination against Catholics continued. Tired of unfair treatment, many Irish wanted complete **separation** from the UK. Finally, in 1916, a small group began a rebellion against the English in order to establish the Irish Republic. They were quickly defeated, but the movement they started was not.

Many Irish politicians promised to separate from the UK if they were elected, and in 1918, their party was voted into power. They supported a group called the Irish Republican Army. The IRA began another rebellion against the English a year later. After two years of war, the two countries signed a peace treaty in 1921. Protestants in the north did not want to leave the UK, and Northern Ireland was created as a result. The rest of Ireland began a journey towards independence.

The situation remained complicated until 1949, when the Republic of Ireland Act finally ended all political connections between Ireland and the UK. Although conflicts continued to exist for years, both Ireland and Northern Ireland are now enjoying a period of peace and stability.

Choose the correct words for the blanks from the highlighted words in the passage.

1. _____ an act of entering a country or an area by force to take control of it
2. _____ an agreement made between countries through negotiation
3. _____ to oppose or disobey some values, policies, or systems of a society
4. _____ to choose a person for a specific position by voting for them
5. _____ to specify sth by a particular title, term, or description

28

1 What is the best title for the passage?

   a. The Story of Irish Independence

   b. The History of Northern Ireland

   c. British Colonies in Western Europe

   d. The Culture and Language of Ireland

DETAILS

2 Write T if the statement is true or F if it's false.

   (1) England and Ireland shared the same religion before the 1500s.   _____

   (2) Irish leaders were satisfied with the conversion to Protestantism.   _____

   (3) A bill introduced in 1800 forced Irish people to move to the UK.   _____

3 What did many Irish politicians promise to do if they were elected?

_____

4 Which is closest in meaning to complicated?

   a. plain   b. intricate   c. worse   d. urgent

5 Put the following information about how Ireland became independent in order.

_____ → _____ → _____ → ⓓ

   ⓐ King Henry VIII changed the religion of England to Protestantism.

   ⓑ The Irish Republican Army and the English fought a war for about two years.

   ⓒ Protestants oppressed Irish people who remained Catholic.

   ⓓ Ireland became a completely independent country.

SUMMARY

6 The sentence below is the first sentence of a short summary of the passage. Choose THREE additional sentences from below to complete the summary.

> Ireland was controlled by England for a long period of time.

   a. Today, Ireland covers a much larger area than Northern Ireland.

   b. English Protestants did not allow Irish Catholics to have equal rights.

   c. Irish landlords owned much of the land in the UK.

   d. There were several attempts by the Irish to rebel against England.

   e. Irish culture was secretly enjoyed by the English even during the war.

   f. Ireland became an independent country, but one area remained part of the UK.

The Tea Act

During the British colonial period, Britain's Parliament imposed many taxes on the American colonies. The colonies had no elected representatives in British Parliament, which meant the colonists weren't treated like British citizens. Many Americans believed it was illegal to tax people without any political rights. The situation grew even worse with
5 the passing of the Tea Act of 1773. This event triggered the beginning of the American Revolution.

Members of Parliament did not realize how angry the Tea Act would make the colonists. The purpose of the Tea Act was to help the East India Company by allowing it to export half a million pounds of tea to the American colonies tax-free. But colonists
10 had been buying tea smuggled from Holland because they didn't like the idea of a British company having a monopoly on tea. Regardless of the cheaper price, they angrily resisted Parliament's Tea Act.

As a form of protest, the colonists decided to boycott tea. Some colonial ports stopped ships carrying British East India Company tea from docking. When ships docked
15 in Boston, patriots wanted to come up with a plan to prevent the tea from being unloaded. Members of a patriotic group named the Sons of Liberty met to decide what action should be taken to send a clear message to Britain.

On the night of December 16, 1773, some members of the Sons of Liberty dressed as Mohawks, a native American tribe, and boarded the ships. They dumped 342 boxes of tea
20 into Boston Harbor. The colonists demonstrated that they were no longer willing to sit by and allow their rights to be ignored.

■ The British response was to pass a set of regulations that became known as the "Intolerable Acts." One of these laws closed Boston Harbor. ■ They were angered by the acts and decided that it was time to fight back. ■ A convention was called and the First
25 Continental Congress was formed. The revolution was about to begin. ■

1 According to paragraph 2, why did the British pass the Tea Act?

ⓐ to impose more taxes on its colonies

ⓑ to support the East India Company's efforts to export tea

ⓒ to encourage colonists to buy tea at a cheaper price

ⓓ to prevent the East India Company from gaining an illegal monopoly

2 The word boycott in the passage is closest in meaning to

(a) collect   (b) transport   (c) exchange   (d) reject

3 All of the following are mentioned as forms of protest by colonists against the Tea Act EXCEPT

(a) declaring a boycott against tea

(b) stopping ships carrying tea from docking

(c) throwing over 300 boxes of tea into Boston Harbor

(d) closing down Boston Harbor

4 Look at the four squares [■] that indicate where the following sentence could be added to the passage.

Americans were told that the harbor would open as soon as they paid for the tea they had destroyed.

Where would the sentence best fit?

5 Directions   Look at the sentence in bold. It is the first sentence of a short summary of the passage. Choose THREE answers to complete the summary. Wrong answer choices use minor ideas from the passage or use information that is not in the passage.

The American colonies complained about their treatment by Britain's Parliament.

(a) Parliament's passage of the Tea Act angered American colonists.

(b) Parliament predicted how upset the colonists would be about the Tea Act.

(c) The Tea Act forced Boston Harbor to close.

(d) Mohawks supported the Sons of Liberty in protesting against the Tea Act.

(e) Colonists fiercely resisted the Tea Act by destroying tea.

(f) The Intolerable Acts led Americans to form the First Continental Congress.

WARM-UP QUESTION • How can artificial intelligence help humans?

Thanks to the recent, rapid developments in artificial intelligence (AI) technologies, AI is now successfully being used to provide mental health assistance and therapy. There are many ways in which AI can be used for patients of all ages. Let's look at a few examples.

5　　Milo is a robot that looks and acts like a real human. It was designed to help children with autism. Milo helps them understand other people's emotions, express empathy, and develop their social skills. By interacting with Milo, they can become more confident in real social situations. Best of all, this robot therapist never expresses frustration, no matter how many times it repeats the same task!

10　　Woebot, a chatbot therapist that operates on computers and mobile devices, is another example. It helps people recognize what triggers negative thoughts in them and keep such thoughts under control. Every day, Woebot sends messages to its users. It asks simple questions like, "How do 15 you feel today?" The AI behind Woebot allows it to remember users' responses and recognize mood changes. Woebot can give suggestions just like a real therapist. In addition, users can feel more **comfortable** knowing that it will never judge them, since it is just an application.

　　Similarly, a virtual therapist called Ellie was designed to help gather behavioral 20 evidence from patients who are suffering from depression or post-traumatic stress disorder. Like Woebot, Ellie isn't judgmental at all, so people can easily open up and share sensitive information with it. While a patient interacts with Ellie, it analyzes things like their facial expressions, gestures, and tone of voice. This data is then transferred to a human doctor who uses it to recommend further treatment or therapy.

25　　Although AI cannot fully replace human therapists, it is a great help to doctors when it comes to collecting and analyzing patient data. Also, patients who struggle to interact socially with others can benefit from therapy provided by AI. As artificial intelligence technology continues to develop, AI therapy is likely to become more and more common.

WORD FOCUS

⟷ Antonyms for
comfortable

troubled
uneasy
unpleasant
awkward

WORD CHECK

Choose the correct words for the blanks from the highlighted words in the passage.

1. _____ to take the place of sth or sb else
2. _____ to stop being shy and frankly talk about one's feelings
3. _____ help given to sb in doing sth
4. _____ the ability to understand how others feel
5. _____ seeming to be real, but not actually existing

READING SKILL

Guessing unknown words in context

Don't stop reading even if you come across a difficult word. Keep on reading and try to identify what part of speech the word belongs to. Then look at what comes before and after the word.

MAIN IDEA

1 **What is the passage mainly about?**

   a. the uses and benefits of AI therapy

   b. the effects of technology on mental health

   c. the risks of using AI technology

   d. AI doctors for physically disabled people

DETAILS

2 **Which is closest in meaning to <u>interacting</u>?**

   a. improving   b. negotiating   c. encouraging   d. communicating

3 **Which is NOT true about Woebot?**

   a. It is an application that works on electronic devices.

   b. It helps users recognize and control their thoughts.

   c. It can recommend therapeutic methods to users.

   d. It judges users based on the feelings that they show.

4 **What was Ellie designed to do?**

_____

5 **Which word best describes the relationship between AI and human therapists?**

   a. identical   b. hierarchical   c. complementary d. alternative

SUMMARY

6 **Use the words in the box to fill in the blanks.**

| frustration | judges | negative | suggestions | transfers | virtual | behavioral |

AI Therapy

Milo	▪ helps provide therapy for children with autism ▪ never expresses _____
Woebot	▪ helps people keep _____ thoughts under control ▪ can give _____ just like a real therapist
Ellie	▪ helps gather _____ evidence ▪ analyzes data and _____ it to a human doctor

WARM-UP QUESTION • Have you heard of "big data"?

A middle school student wants to buy a new pair of jeans and has been comparing prices online. To her surprise, she receives an email advertising a special sale on jeans from one of the websites that she visited. Soon after, she sees a banner advertisement for that same website while surfing the Internet. How could this be? It is all because of "big data"—a revolution in the way that customer data is being collected and utilized.

These days, it is not hard for companies to gather huge amounts of customer data. What's difficult is putting it all to good use. When _____(A)_____, big data can show patterns and trends that can be useful in predicting what a shopper will be interested in. In other words, big data is less about huge increases in storage capacity and more about improved statistical and computational methods that actually make all of this data useful.

One example of a company making the best use of big data is Amazon.com. Amazon keeps track of what items people purchase on their website, which items are in a shopper's virtual shopping cart, and even which items they have only viewed. Then, it uses this data to provide customers with a personalized shopping experience. As soon as shoppers return to the website, they are shown both items that they have already considered purchasing and items that Amazon predicts that they will be interested in. In fact, 29% of Amazon's sales now come through these recommendations.

But there are also concerns about big data, both for the customers whose data is being collected and for the companies trying to use it. One of the biggest issues is privacy because data is often sold to third parties without the customers knowing. Also, companies like Amazon depend on Internet search terms, but these can be misleading because the words that people search are not always related to what they would like to purchase. In spite of these problems, it is clear that big data has revolutionized the way that individuals interact with the online world.

WORD FOCUS

⊜ Synonyms for
predict

forecast
anticipate
foresee

WORD CHECK

Choose the correct words for the blanks from the highlighted words in the passage.

1. _____ designed for a specific user
2. _____ to make use of sth
3. _____ sth that causes worry
4. _____ a general movement or tendency
5. _____ giving the wrong idea or a false impression

READING SKILL

Inferring from the context

To effectively understand a passage, we sometimes need to infer facts that are not mentioned. Some writers leave key points out of the passage and expect readers to infer them. Understanding exactly what the author is trying to say is important.

MAIN IDEA

1 **What is the best title for the passage?**

a. The Risks of Online Shopping

b. The Key to the Success of Amazon.com

c. Big Data: A New Way of Advertising

d. Big Data: Revolutionizing the Online World

DETAILS

2 **What is the best expression for blank (A)?**

a. freely shared

b. carelessly stored

c. properly analyzed

d. illegally collected

3 **Which is closest in meaning to keeps track of?**

a. monitors   b. expects   c. consists of   d. controls

4 **Why is privacy one of the biggest concerns about big data according to paragraph 4?**

_____

5 **Which is NOT true about big data according to the passage?**

a. It enables companies to predict what a shopper would like to buy.

b. Customer data is utilized through statistical and computational methods.

c. It can be used to offer personalized services to Internet shoppers.

d. It can mislead customers into buying unnecessary items.

SUMMARY

6 Use the words in the box to fill in the blanks.

| privacy   sales   unrelated   purchase   analyze   recommendations   similar |

Big data refers to new ways in which companies collect and _____ information about their customers. It helps them predict what items their customers will _____. This increases their sales and provides customers with a unique shopping experience. For example, Amazon.com uses big data to provide returning customers with product _____. But there are also problems with big data, including questions of _____ and search terms that are _____ to what customers actually want to buy.

35

WORD REVIEW TEST

[1~3] Choose the word that is closest in meaning to the underlined word.

1. She encouraged her students to participate in the contest.
    a. agreed   b. donated   c. introduced   d. motivated

2. After the accident, movement in his left arm was restricted.
    a. banned   b. limited   c. permitted   d. connected

3. The government is blamed for ignoring the country's economic crisis.
    a. solving   b. worrying   c. overlooking   d. realizing

[4~7] Connect the matching words in columns A and B.

A		B
4. sign •	•	a. an army
5. defeat •	•	b. regional products
6. impose •	•	c. a peace treaty
7. export •	•	d. a tax

[8~11] Choose the best word to complete each sentence.

8. Some people think it's impossible to eliminate racial _____ completely.
    a. invasions   b. influence   c. difficulties   d. discrimination

9. Barack Obama was _____ as the first African-American president of the US.
    a. represented   b. demonstrated   c. elected   d. rebelled

10. The incident on the border _____ a war between the two countries.
    a. converted   b. triggered   c. destroyed   d. resisted

11. It is _____ to drive without a driver's license.
    a. official   b. illegal   c. intolerable   d. complicated

[12~14] Choose the correct word for each definition.

boycott   patriot   adopt   act   monopoly   exist

12. to be present in a particular situation or place:

13. a law that has been passed by the government:

14. to refuse to buy or use something as a protest:

[1~4] Choose the word that is closest in meaning to the underlined word.

1. Many citizens raised <u>concerns</u> about the issue of hate crime.
    a. interests   b. questions   c. thoughts   d. worries

2. The company received financial <u>assistance</u> from the government.
    a. aid   b. control   c. response   d. disturbance

3. The students spent a few days <u>gathering</u> the information for their assignment.
    a. storing   b. revising   c. collecting   d. comprehending

4. They accepted the waiter's <u>recommendation</u> for what to order.
    a. intention   b. demand   c. application   d. suggestion

[5~8] Connect the matching words in columns A and B.

A		B
5. surf •		• a. various people
6. transfer •		• b. the Internet
7. interact with •		• c. empathy
8. express •		• d. patient data

[9~12] Choose the best word to complete each sentence. (Change the form if needed.)

analyze   capacity   privacy   purchase   replace   intelligence

9. Many factory workers could be _____ by robots in the near future.

10. He regarded entering his room without permission as an invasion of _____.

11. We will exchange the existing fuel tank for one with a(n) _____ of 100 liters.

12. The scientist is _____ the results of the experiment.

[13~16] Choose the correct word for each definition.

pattern   disorder   revolutionize   statistical   struggle   artificial   judgmental

13. created by humans:

14. a regular, repeated order or arrangement of something:

15. criticizing others' behavior or opinions too quickly:

16. to completely change the way people act or think:

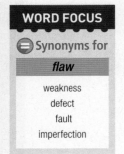

Do you feel as though you don't deserve your success? If so, you could be experiencing the imposter syndrome. It's a strong feeling that you aren't really as competent as others think

5 you are. Instead, you feel like an imposter. It's not an uncommon feeling—even Albert Einstein worried that his work was getting more attention than it deserved. However, it can lead to negative consequences. People with this syndrome have difficulty sharing their ideas or pursuing challenging goals.

10   The imposter syndrome was first noticed in the 1970s, by psychologists Pauline Clance and Suzanne Imes. They found that many of their female students felt they didn't deserve to be enrolled at their college. Based on a hypothesis that only high-achieving women are affected by this syndrome, they conducted more research. They realized that it was a widespread issue regardless of age, race, and gender.

15   There isn't a single cause of the imposter syndrome. However, many people who suffer from it share the same personality trait—perfectionism. In their minds, only people without **flaw**s deserve success. It is actually natural to focus on one's own flaws because the human brain is hardwired to pay closer attention to negative things, which it considers a threat.

20   The best way to deal with the imposter syndrome is simply by talking. ⓐ People struggling with it are usually afraid to ask others about their performance. ⓑ They worry that they will find out that they really are a fraud. ⓒ When they open up and discuss their fears and doubts, they are likely to find out that they really do deserve their success. ⓓ What's more, they will realize that they are not the only ones who feel like imposters.

25   There is no way to make the imposter syndrome go away forever. However, _____(A)_____ can control these negative feelings and prevent them from becoming overwhelming.

WORD FOCUS

⊜ Synonyms for

flaw

weakness
defect
fault
imperfection

Choose the correct words for the blanks from the highlighted words in the passage.

1. _____ having enough skill or ability to do sth
2. _____ possible danger
3. _____ sth that follows as a result
4. _____ sb who pretends to be sb else in order to deceive others
5. _____ happening or existing in many places or among many people

1 What is the passage mainly about?

    a. a condition that causes feelings of self-doubt

    b. traits of people who pretend to be someone else

    c. the reason why people are proud of their success

    d. features of perfectionism and its side effects

2 According to paragraph 1, what difficulty do people with the imposter syndrome have?

_____

3 Which is NOT mentioned about the imposter syndrome?

    a. who started studying it

    b. who might suffer from it

    c. why it draws attention from scientists

    d. how it can be handled

4 Where would the following sentence best fit in paragraph 4?

> But the opposite is actually true.

5 What is the best expression for blank (A)?

    a. overestimating your abilities   b. focusing on challenging goals

    c. communicating openly and honestly   d. analyzing your strengths and weaknesses

6 Use the words in the box to fill in the blanks.

> negative   success   openly   perfectionists   unworthy   talented   psychologists

The Imposter Syndrome

- Definition: a feeling that you aren't as _____ as other people believe
- First studied by Pauline Clance and Suzanne Imes
  - noticed students considered themselves _____ of their college
- Most commonly suffered by _____
- Best way to deal with it: talking _____
  - accept that they do deserve their _____
  - realize other people feel the same way

WARM-UP QUESTION • What is the most important factor when you buy something?

Many people think that they make purchasing decisions on their own. But in fact, there are several psychological factors that influence one's opinion of a product. The two strongest of these factors are called the "primacy effect" and the "recency effect."

⁵ The primacy effect is the strong **impression** left on a consumer by the first information that he or she receives about a certain product. Imagine that you first find out about a product in a commercial that presents the product as being exciting and revolutionary. This information is more likely to stick in your mind than other information that comes immediately after.

The recency effect, though, is considered to be even stronger. It is the impression ¹⁰ made by the last information received about an item. So, if you hear some negative reviews after having a positive first impression, the recency effect takes over, and

_____ (A) _____. These two powerful effects overshadow what you learn between your first and last impressions. As a result, large amounts of information have little effect on the opinion you form.

WORD FOCUS

◀ Collocations for

impression

overall *impression*
initial *impression*
give an *impression*
get an *impression*

¹⁵ Marketers are very aware of this. To assure a good first impression, they try to promote products through print, radio, television, and Internet advertising before there is any chance of them being reviewed negatively. They also try to control the recency effect by designing packaging that makes their product look sophisticated and appealing. They hope that this final positive impression erases any previous negative opinion a consumer ²⁰ might have had.

This means that much of the research you do about a product ends up being wiped away by marketing. So what can you do? If there is something you want, search for reliable sources like customer reviews without looking at any advertisements. This will allow you to form educated ²⁵ opinions before being controlled by advertising tactics. As a result, you can be sure to make good purchasing decisions.

WORD CHECK

Choose the correct words for the blanks from the highlighted words in the passage.

1. _____ to make sth else less noticeable
2. _____ to encourage the buying of sth
3. _____ new and completely different
4. _____ related to the mind and thought processes
5. _____ well designed and highly advanced

MAIN IDEA

1 **What is the passage mainly about?**

a. different advertising tactics for different products

b. the importance of others' opinions about a product

c. the influence of attractive packaging design on product sales

d. psychological factors that influence purchasing decisions

Identifying the main idea

When you recognize the main idea of a passage, you can focus on what is important and skim over other information. It's common for an author to mention the main idea in the first paragraph and repeat it again in the conclusion.

DETAILS

2 According to paragraph 2, what is the primacy effect?

_____

3 What is the best expression for blank (A)?

a. your first impression stays the same

b. your impression becomes negative

c. the primacy effect gets in the way

d. it makes the positive impression even stronger

4 Who was most likely affected by the recency effect, based on the passage?

> Tom: I bought these shoes on impulse because they were 40% off.
> Britney: I bought this bag as soon as I saw it advertised.
> Mark: I bought this watch because my brother highly recommended it.
> Jay: I was going to buy a smartphone, but I decided not to after reading a bad review.

a. Tom   b. Britney   c. Mark   d. Jay

5 Write T if the statement is true or F if it's false.

(1) The recency effect is related to a person's first impression of a product.   _____

(2) Marketers use a variety of tactics to give consumers a positive impression.   _____

(3) Attractive packaging cannot reverse consumers' prior impressions of
   a product.   _____

SUMMARY

6 Use the words in the box to fill in the blanks.

> previously   influence   recently   psychological   research   first   advertise

There are two key _____ factors that affect whether or not a consumer decides to purchase a certain item. The primacy effect is the impression left by the _____ information received about a particular product. The recency effect is the impression made by the most _____ acquired information about a product. Marketers know that these have a lot of _____, so they try to control them. Therefore, you should _____ products on your own to make wise purchases.

One day, a fifteen-year-old Pakistani girl named Malala Yousafzai was riding a bus home from school. Suddenly, a man from a group called the Taliban got on the bus and **attack**ed her, nearly killing her. People all over the world were shocked and wondered why a young girl would be the target of such an attack.

Malala's town in Pakistan had been under constant threat from Taliban soldiers, who had forbidden girls from going to school. Malala had written for a BBC News blog, describing what daily life was like under such conditions. She had also written about what a great loss it was for Pakistan to have so many young girls not attending school. The Taliban were very angry at her for this. Miraculously, Malala survived the attack. Since then, her voice has only become stronger as she has continued fighting to _____(A)_____ in Pakistan.

Unfortunately, almost half of the girls in Pakistan have never been to school or have dropped out. Without proper education and training, these girls will never have an equal opportunity to achieve great things in their lives. But thanks to Malala's brave actions, people's attitudes in Pakistan are changing. They are now realizing the importance of education for girls, and the government has started to make efforts to increase the participation of girls in primary schools.

But a lack of education is not just a problem in Pakistan. Around the globe, there are millions of girls who are <u>prevented</u> from going to school. That is why Malala started the Malala Fund, a charity whose goal is to make it possible for girls all over the world to access education. The Malala Fund supports educators and activists in order to raise awareness and provide opportunities to girls worldwide.

Now, thanks to Malala's bravery and passion, people all over the world are acknowledging the importance of education. We should all follow Malala's lead and unite to make sure that every child in the world gets the education that he or she deserves.

WORD FOCUS

⟷ Antonyms for

attack

protect
guard
secure

WORD CHECK

Choose the correct words for the blanks from the highlighted words in the passage.

1. _____ the act of taking part in sth
2. _____ present at all times; unending and continuous
3. _____ to come together in a peaceful and cooperative way
4. _____ an organization that helps people in need
5. _____ to successfully do sth

1 What is the best title for the passage?
   a. Malala Yousafzai: A Survivor of an Attack
   b. Malala Yousafzai: A Hope for Pakistani People
   c. Malala Yousafzai: An End to Misery in Pakistan
   d. Malala Yousafzai: A Brave Voice for Education

2 What is the best expression for blank (A)?
   a. improve education for girls
   b. prevent terrorist attacks
   c. launch a campaign against war
   d. offer quality work experience

3 What has the government of Pakistan started thanks to Malala's brave actions?

_____

4 Which is closest in meaning to <u>prevented</u>?
   a. investigated   b. encouraged   c. stopped   d. postponed

5 Which of the following is NOT true according to the passage?
   a. Malala was nearly killed in a Taliban attack.
   b. Malala's town was under continuous threat from the Taliban.
   c. Malala wrote on her blog about the attack she experienced on the bus.
   d. Malala also works to help educate girls in other countries.

6 Use the words in the box to fill in the blanks.

| threat   participation   special   educational   permitted   forbidden   bravery |

Malala Yousafzai wrote for the BBC blog that described daily life in her town in Pakistan. Her town was under constant military _____ from the Taliban, who had _____ girls from going to school. The Taliban attacked her, but she survived. Now she has become a globally recognized voice for the promotion of girls' education. Thanks to Malala's _____, Pakistan's attitude toward education is changing, and now her Malala Fund is helping to provide _____ opportunities for girls all over the world.

Tonight, 14-year-old Wolfgang is getting his tools ready. Tomorrow is his first day of training at a computer company. For the next three weeks, Wolfgang will not attend classes at his vocational high school. Instead, he will get work

5 experience that will help him become a *meister*, or "master," computer technician. Anna, his ten-year-old sister, is busy studying in the next room. She goes to a different school than her brother. At her school, all of the students are planning to eventually attend university.

Wolfgang and Anna live in Germany. When children enter elementary school there,

10 they stay with the same group of students and the same teacher for four years. At the end of the fourth year, students are evaluated based upon their school records and natural abilities. They can then attend either an academic school to prepare for university or a vocational school to learn a trade.

This system of education is quite different from those of Asian countries. In Japan,

15 for example, students take competitive examinations throughout their school years. These examinations determine which junior high school, high school, and college they can attend. In Germany, on the other hand, students' futures are largely decided by the time they finish the fourth grade of elementary school.

Students in Germany seem happy with the system. Many feel that the lack of

20 competitive tests creates a less stressful environment. "I'd rather focus on something I love, like computers, than other subjects, like history and biology," says Wolfgang. The work experience he'll get at a company before he finishes high school will allow him to get a good job in the future.

The German education system benefits both the individual and the country.

25 Students are able to focus on their particular interests and natural abilities. After they graduate, they can then apply these skills in ways that earn them money while making the national **economy** stronger.

WORD FOCUS

🔍 Collocations for

economy

global *economy*
local *economy*
world *economy*
market *economy*

**WORD
CHECK**

Choose the correct words for the blanks from the highlighted words in the passage.

1. _____ for the most part
2. _____ a specific kind of job that requires special training
3. _____ relating to job or career skills
4. _____ to measure a person's performance
5. _____ sb who works with electrical instruments, such as computers

MAIN IDEA

1 What aspect of German education does the passage mainly discuss?
   a. the quality of the classes
   b. the superiority of vocational education
   c. requirements for getting into college
   d. the system of respecting students' individuality

DETAILS

2 How are students evaluated at the end of their fourth year of elementary school?

_____

3 How does the current German education system benefit the country according to paragraph 5?
   a. It promotes economic growth.
   b. It attracts foreign students.
   c. It reduces the education budget.
   d. It increases the competitiveness of universities.

4 Which of the following is true according to the passage?
   a. In Germany, students start to consider their careers in high school.
   b. German academic schools are more competitive than those in Asia.
   c. In Japan, students don't have to take a junior high school entrance exam.
   d. German students in vocational schools are given job training opportunities.

SUMMARY

5 Match each topic to the correct paragraph in the passage.
   (1) Paragraph 1 •   • ⓐ a description of the German education system
   (2) Paragraph 2 •   • ⓑ an introduction to two typical German students
   (3) Paragraph 3 •   • ⓒ students' opinions of the German education system
   (4) Paragraph 4 •   • ⓓ a comparison between the German and Japanese
                                education systems
   (5) Paragraph 5 •   • ⓔ individual and national benefits of the German
                                education system

WORD REVIEW TEST

[1~4] Choose the word that is closest in meaning to the underlined word.

1. New policies were introduced to <u>deal with</u> the unemployment problem.
    a. open up   b. cope with   c. take over   d. end up

2. Her books have greatly <u>influenced</u> the imagination of children around the world.
    a. restricted   b. completed   c. accepted   d. affected

3. As science developed, many <u>revolutionary</u> inventions were created.
    a. effective   b. innovative   c. uncommon   d. ambiguous

4. Thousands of people had lost their homes as a <u>consequence</u> of the typhoon.
    a. cause   b. destruction   c. result   d. preparation

[5~8] Connect the matching words in columns A and B.

A		B
5. design •		• a. a local college
6. pursue •		• b. one's feelings
7. control •		• c. a product
8. be enrolled at •		• d. a challenging goal

[9~12] Choose the best word to complete each sentence. (Change the form if needed.)

stick   erase   opposite   appealing   promote   fraud

9. The word "positive" is the _____ of "negative."

10. The painting has _____ in my mind since I saw it.

11. He wanted to _____ the tragic memory of that night.

12. The product was _____ through TV advertisements.

[13~16] Choose the correct word for each definition.

commercial   previous   tactic   hypothesis   factor   flaw   performance

13. a fault or weakness that makes someone or something imperfect:

14. a statement that has not been proved by scientific research:

15. a television or radio advertisement:

16. a specific method or strategy used to accomplish a goal:

[1~4] Choose the word that is closest in meaning to the underlined word.

1. Most airlines <u>forbid</u> the use of cell phones during takeoff.
   a. ban   b. refuse   c. replace   d. disprove

2. I sometimes feel depressed for no <u>particular</u> reason.
   a. reasonable   b. normal   c. natural   d. specific

3. My grandfather recently started to study English at an <u>elementary</u> level.
   a. basic   b. compulsory   c. secondary   d. complicated

4. We must <u>acknowledge</u> that we can't fix this problem.
   a. solve   b. overlook   c. analyze   d. recognize

[5~8] Connect the matching words in columns A and B.

A		B
5. survive •		• a. university
6. make •		• b. an effort
7. attend •		• c. confident
8. seem •		• d. a disaster

[9~12] Choose the best word to complete each sentence. (Change the form if needed.)

technician	competitive	deserve	opportunity	increase	determine

9. She doesn't _____ to be treated so unfairly.

10. Your future is not _____ by just a single college entrance exam.

11. We need to call a _____ who can repair this laptop.

12. A student exchange program is a great _____ to experience foreign cultures.

[13~16] Choose the correct word for each definition.

attitude	master	apply	target	passion	trade

13. very strong enthusiasm for something:

14. the way people think, feel, or behave:

15. to put to use, especially for a particular purpose:

16. someone who is extremely skilled at a particular activity:

When people hear the word "cork," they usually think about wine. This is because 70% of cork is used to make bottle stoppers. But cork can be used to make many things, including musical instruments and floor tiles. What's more, using cork has a minimal **impact** on the environment.

Cork trees grow in many Mediterranean countries, such as Spain, Italy, and Algeria. Portugal, the world's top cork producer, closely regulates the harvesting of cork. Cork trees cannot be harvested until they are at least 25 years old. After that, harvesting can only take place once every nine years.

Cork trees are not cut down when they are harvested. _____(A)_____, the outer layer of their bark is peeled away. This does not kill the trees. In fact, they can keep living for another 170 years or more. There is also another benefit to this method. When trees are regrowing their bark, they absorb five times more carbon dioxide than they usually do. Carbon dioxide is one of the greenhouse gases that is causing the earth to heat up. _____(B)_____, removing it from the atmosphere can help slow down climate change.

After the cork is harvested, it is transported to a factory. There, it is dried and boiled, and then turned into various products. These cork factories are also environmentally friendly. Manufacturing cork products leaves behind lots of cork dust. The factories burn this dust to create up to 90% of the energy they use.

Of all the cork that is removed from trees, almost none is wasted. The cork used to make bottle stoppers can even be recycled into a variety of products, from sports balls to engine parts. Therefore, we can say that growing cork trees helps protect our planet. For these reasons, many people consider cork to be a nearly perfect material.

WORD FOCUS

◀ Collocations for
impact

major _impact_
social _impact_
direct _impact_
negative _impact_

WORD CHECK

Choose the correct words for the blanks from the highlighted words in the passage.

1. _____ to move sth from one location to another
2. _____ to take in
3. _____ very small in amount or degree
4. _____ to gather crops from a field
5. _____ one of multiple sheets of material covering a surface

1   What is the best title for the passage?

    a. Strict Regulations of Cork Harvesting
    b. Cork: The Environmentally Friendly Material
    c. Cork: The Perfect Material for Bottle Stoppers
    d. The Advantages and Disadvantages of Growing Cork Trees

DETAILS

2   Which is the closest in meaning to regulates?

    a. reduces   b. generates   c. controls   d. prohibits

3   What is the best pair for blanks (A) and (B)?

	(A)	(B)
a.	In contrast	In other words
b.	Instead	Therefore
c.	In addition	As a result
d.	Otherwise	However

4   According to paragraph 4, why are cork factories environmentally friendly?

    _____

5   Which is NOT true about the cork trees?

    a. In Portugal, they can be harvested before they are 25 years old.
    b. The harvesting method of peeling their bark ensures their survival.
    c. They take in lots of carbon dioxide while regrowing their bark.
    d. They can be used to make various products including bottle stoppers.

SUMMARY

6   Use the words in the box to fill in the blanks.

planted dust harvested peeled regrowing barks layers

Cork trees are grown in the Mediterranean region. The trees are _____ without being cut down. Instead, their bark is _____ away, a procedure that does not kill them. When the trees are _____ their bark, they remove more carbon dioxide from the atmosphere. Cork factories are also environmentally friendly, as they burn cork _____ as an energy source. For these reasons and more, cork can be considered a nearly perfect material.

WARM-UP QUESTION • What do you like best about your city?

"Cities are not the problem, they are the solution." This sentence was spoken by Jaime Lerner, the former mayor of a Brazilian city named Curitiba. Since the 1950s, Curitiba has been a model city for urban planning, which is the science of designing cities to make them more **convenient** and practical. When Lerner became
5 mayor in the 1970s, he took this concept further, making Curitiba a green city by taking environmentally friendly steps.

One of the most notable features of Curitiba is its large amount of green space. Despite the fact that the city's population has tripled in the past 20 years, there are more than 1,000 public green spaces including man-made parks and forests. This is because
10 the city has strict laws protecting local vegetation from development.

But perhaps Curitiba's most effective project is its Green Exchange program, introduced in 1991. Under the program, low-income families can exchange bags of trash for useful items, such as bus tickets and food. When children bring in recyclable goods, they receive school supplies, chocolate and toys in return. Because of this program and
15 other similar ones, approximately 70% of the city's trash is recycled, which reduces the impact on landfills and keeps the streets clean.

Finally, Curitiba's bus system has played a large role in making the city a better place to live. Some of the buses are long and split into three sections like a
20 train. This allows each vehicle to carry more people, reducing both traffic and carbon emissions. What's more, there's only one price for a bus ticket no matter how far you travel. This attracts more riders, greatly reducing the number of private automobiles on the road and thereby lowering fuel consumption.

25 Curitiba is often called _____(A)_____, but it didn't get this title just by luck. It was earned through the careful planning and innovative programs of the city's government, along with the hard work and cooperation of Curitiba's citizens.

WORD FOCUS
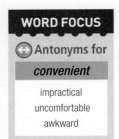

⟷ Antonyms for
convenient

impractical
uncomfortable
awkward

WORD CHECK

Choose the correct words for the blanks from the highlighted words in the passage.

1. _____ to increase by three times
2. _____ a release of sth like smoke
3. _____ to divide sth
4. _____ an act of using sth
5. _____ firm and inflexible

1 What is the passage mainly about?

a. who started an urban planning project in Curitiba
b. how Curitiba increased its green space
c. what makes Curitiba such a green city
d. why Curitiba's bus system has been copied by other cities

2 Which is closest in meaning to notable?

a. remarkable   b. precise   c. extensive   d. appropriate

3 How can low-income families participate in the Green Exchange program according to paragraph 3?

_____

4 Which is NOT mentioned about Curitiba's bus system?

a. As its buses are designed to carry more people, it helps ease traffic.
b. It attracts more citizens to use it by charging a single fare.
c. It decreases the use of private cars, leading to less fuel consumption.
d. It benefits low-income families by making buses available free of charge to them.

5 What is the best expression for blank (A)?

a. the most crowded city in Brazil
b. a city of high fuel consumption
c. one of the most sustainable cities on Earth
d. a simple solution for recycling materials

6 Use the words in the box to fill in the blanks.

| rising   recycling   private   traffic   public   exchange   development |

Curitiba, the Green City

- green space: local vegetation legally protected from _____
  → large number of _____ green spaces
- Green Exchange program: poor people given useful items in _____ for trash
  → high _____ rates, cleaner streets
- bus system: long buses and one-price tickets
  → less _____, pollution and fuel use

UNIT

10

Geology

READING 1

WARM-UP QUESTION • Can you name any famous volcanoes?

Watching a volcano erupt can be amazing, but it is also very dangerous. Although other natural disasters, such as floods and earthquakes, kill far more people each year, volcanoes remain a serious **threat** in many parts of the world.

There are two basic kinds of eruptions. The key difference between the two is how sticky the magma is. If the magma is thin, like water, it is easy for gas to escape from it. Therefore, an explosive eruption is unlikely to occur. This is the situation in Hawaii. Hot lava sometimes flows over the edges of Hawaii's famous volcanoes, but it rarely does much damage and is easy to predict.

Some volcanoes, on the other hand, contain magma that is very thick. The gas bubbles that form within it are unable to escape, so pressure builds up over time. Eventually, the magma explodes in a violent eruption. These eruptions are quite dangerous and difficult to predict. Most famous eruptions, such as the one that destroyed ancient Pompeii and the one that occurred at Mount St. Helens in 1980, were of this type.

In recent years, however, scientists have been experimenting with different ways to predict when eruptions will occur and how strong they will be. One of their most reliable methods is to measure the shaking of the volcano. When magma travels upward from deep in the earth, it causes thousands of tiny earthquakes. When the number of these earthquakes increases, scientists know an eruption is drawing closer. There are other methods as well, including analyzing the gases rising from the volcano, measuring the angle of its slopes, and even observing the behavior of animals in the area.

Predicting eruptions is important work, but it can also be extremely dangerous. Ten scientists were killed in 1993 when a Colombian volcano they were investigating erupted unexpectedly. To prevent such tragedies, most of the activities used to predict eruptions are now done from a safe distance. Although it remains difficult to predict exactly when an eruption will occur, scientists hope that continuous research will someday make this possible.

WORD FOCUS

◀ Collocations for

threat

great *threat*
constant *threat*
pose *a threat*
receive *a threat*

WORD CHECK

Choose the correct words for the blanks from the highlighted words in the passage.

1. _____ to completely break or ruin sth
2. _____ the way sth is done
3. _____ hot melted rock that emerges from a volcano
4. _____ an area of land that exists at an angle
5. _____ to explode outward

READING SKILL

Identifying cause and effect
To recognize cause and effect, we look for words and phrases such as 'because,' 'consequently,' 'so that,' and 'as a result.' We can then identify how the information fits together in the passage. Start with a "why" question to discover the cause and then try to find the effect.

MAIN IDEA

1 **What is the passage mainly about?**

   a. natural disasters that threaten lives
   b. famous volcanoes and the damage they caused
   c. types of volcanic eruptions and how they are predicted
   d. new technology used to predict eruptions

DETAILS

2 **Why do volcanoes containing thick magma explode violently according to paragraph 3?**

   _____

3 **Which is NOT mentioned as a way to predict volcanic eruptions?**

   a. observing an increasing number of earthquakes
   b. analyzing the gas coming from a volcano
   c. studying how animals' behavior changes
   d. recording how many eruptions occur in the area

4 **Why does the writer mention the eruption of a Colombian volcano in paragraph 5?**

   a. to demonstrate the danger of trying to predict volcanic eruptions
   b. to explain the reason why predicting eruptions is important
   c. to compare it with other eruptions in the past
   d. to discuss how to escape a volcanic eruption safely

SUMMARY

5 **Use the words in the box to fill in the blanks.**

   | bubbles   predicting   slopes   explosive   observing   thin   distance |

   Volcanic Eruptions

   - **Two main types**
     - _____ magma → gas escapes → mild eruption
     - thick magma → gas is trapped → _____ eruption
   - **Methods of predicting eruptions**
     - monitoring the shaking of the volcano
     - analyzing gases
     - measuring the volcano's _____
     - _____ animals
   - **Caution in investigating volcanoes**
     - Scientists try to predict eruptions from a safe _____.

← → C

Lunar Sample 14321 🔍

In 1971, NASA's Apollo 14 mission landed on the surface of the moon. After taking photos and conducting some research, the astronauts collected moon rocks to bring back to Earth.

One of these rocks is now getting a lot of attention. It is a nine-kilogram rock about
5 the size of a basketball, officially known as sample 14321. This rock may have formed on Earth about 4 billion years ago. If so, it would be the oldest Earth rock ever found.

The rock is made up of many small pieces stuck together. Most of them are dark and seem to be typical lunar material. One piece, however, is brighter than the rest and contains zircon, a mineral that is more commonly found on Earth than on the moon. Scientists
10 analyzed the chemistry of the zircon and concluded that the piece found in sample 14321 formed in relatively cool, oxygen-rich magma that had been subjected to high pressure. These conditions are extremely rare on the moon. It's more likely that it formed about 20 kilometers beneath Earth's surface approximately 4 billion years ago. At that time, Earth's conditions would have closely matched the ones in which the piece is thought to have
15 formed.

But how did it end up on the moon? Billions of years ago, Earth was constantly being hit by asteroids and meteorites. ■ Over time, these impacts may have driven the rock closer and closer to Earth's surface. ■ This assumption is plausible because the moon was three times closer to Earth than it is today. ■ Later, another impact may have brought it up onto
20 the moon's surface, where it remained until an astronaut picked it up. ■

Sample 14321 could provide scientists with vital information about the geologic conditions on early Earth. It is also possible that there are rocks from other planets, such as Mars and Venus, on the moon's surface. These too would likely provide scientists with valuable data about the early solar system.

1 What is the best title for the passage?

ⓐ Did the Moon Originally Form on Earth?

ⓑ A Moon Rock with Surprising Origins

ⓒ The Unusual Qualities of Lunar Material

ⓓ The Biggest Collision Ever on Earth

2 Sample 14321 is getting lots of attention because

(a) it was collected by NASA's Apollo 14 mission.

(b) it contains minerals that are rare on Earth.

(c) it might be the oldest rock formed on Earth.

(d) it consists of many tiny pieces of lunar material.

3 The word subjected in the passage is closest in meaning to

(a) collided   (b) exposed   (c) exploded   (d) connected

4 Look at the four squares [■] that indicate where the following sentence could be added to the passage.

Finally, a huge collision could have sent it flying through space until it crashed into the moon and was buried there.

Where would the sentence best fit?

5 In paragraph 5, the writer mentions Mars and Venus

(a) to show how far away they are from the moon

(b) to explain that their environments are different from Earth's

(c) to emphasize the scientific value of the moon

(d) to describe the possible existence of life on them

6 ▮Directions▮ Look at the sentence in bold. It is the first sentence of a short summary of the passage. Choose THREE answers to complete the summary. Wrong answer choices use minor ideas from the passage or use information that is not in the passage.

The Apollo 14 mission collected many samples of moon rocks in 1971.

(a) Apollo 14 astronauts also took pictures of the moon and did some research.

(b) One rock sample is thought to have formed on Earth billions of years ago.

(c) Sample 14321 may have flown from Earth to the moon after an asteroid impact.

(d) Magma that experiences high levels of pressure contains a lot of oxygen.

(e) The moon may have formed when two other planets crashed together.

(f) Other rocks on the moon might be able to teach us about other planets.

WORD REVIEW TEST

[1~2] Choose the word that is closest in meaning to the underlined word.

1. Bobby is taking private Korean lessons.
    a. common   b. comfortable   c. beneficial   d. individual

2. Strong materials, such as concrete and steel, are necessary for construction.
    a. possessions   b. substances   c. packages   d. weapons

[3~5] Connect the matching words in columns A and B.

A		B
3. protect •		• a. effective steps
4. absorb •		• b. endangered species
5. take •		• c. carbon dioxide

[6~8] Choose the best word to complete each sentence.

6. It would be easier to finish the task if there were _____ among our team members.
    a. cooperation   b. consumption   c. vegetation   d. exchange

7. Online shopping malls provide people with a _____ way to purchase items.
    a. minimal   b. similar   c. convenient   d. strict

8. The _____ trash can be turned into useful items.
    a. notable   b. practical   c. innovative   d. recyclable

[9~11] Circle the odd one out in each group.

9.	tool	source	instrument	device
10.	impact	influence	affection	effect
11.	gather	reap	harvest	distribute

[12~13] Choose the correct definition of the underlined word in each sentence.

> **feature** *n.* **1.** a special point or quality of something: *The best feature of the painting is its vivid color.* **2.** a part of someone's face like the eyes or nose: *He is a young man with fine features.* **3.** a special article or report: *There is a feature on education in this issue.*

12. Beautiful streets are one of the best features of this city.   _____

13. He is writing a feature on the issue of child labor.   _____

[1~4] Choose the word that is closest in meaning to the underlined word.

1. I'm looking for a reliable travel agency.
   a. local   b. capable   c. historical   d. dependable

2. Two cars were badly damaged in the collision.
   a. pressure   b. crash   c. distance   d. condition

3. Snow is not a typical occurrence at this time of year.
   a. unusual   b. man-made   c. normal   d. existent

4. The fingerprints left on the safe didn't match the suspect's.
   a. compete with   b. cover up   c. make up   d. correspond with

[5~8] Connect the matching words in columns A and B.

A		B
5. pick up •		• a. research
6. measure •		• b. a disaster
7. conduct •		• c. the angle of a slope
8. predict •		• d. a pebble on the beach

[9~12] Choose the best word to complete each sentence. (Change the form if needed.)

erupt	violent	sticky	plausible	prevent	observe

9. He had a quite _____ excuse, but no one believed it.

10. A volcano _____ and killed more than 6,000 people.

11. Auroras have been _____ since ancient times.

12. Spiders capture their prey by using _____ webs.

[13~16] Choose the correct word for each definition.

earthquake	lava	escape	surface	attention	assumption

13. something that is thought to be true without definite proof:

14. the top layer of something:

15. to get away from a place or container:

16. a sudden shaking or trembling of the land:

WARM-UP QUESTION • Do you know any countries with unique cultures?

Imagine an eagle that has a wingspan of two meters and can fly at speeds of more than 300 kilometers per hour. Now imagine hunting with it. This is what the Kazakhs, the largest minority in Mongolia, have been doing for centuries. Hunting with golden eagles is a way of life for them.

5　　It starts with an important ritual—capturing and training golden eagles. ⓐ The birds are caught when they are still young, and females are preferred over males, as they are larger and more **aggressive**. ⓑ As a part of the training, hoods are placed over their heads, and their owners spend hours singing to them. ⓒ Golden eagles can live up to 40 years, but they are only kept by hunters for about 10. ⓓ After that, they are released
10　back into the wild.

　　The Kazakhs normally hunt in winter, despite temperatures as low as -40 °C. The white snow makes it easier for the eagles to spot their prey, such as rabbits and foxes. The fur of these animals, important material for the Kazakhs' winter clothing, is also thickest at this time of year. Along with fur, eagle hunting traditionally provided meat for the
15　nomadic Kazakhs. In the past, this skill was passed down from fathers to sons. Today, however, some young Kazakh women learn it as well.

　　In order to promote Kazakh culture to the next generation and around the world, the Golden Eagle Festival has been held since 1999. About 100 hunters participate each year, making it one of the Kazakh's largest annual gatherings. There is a parade, followed
20　by competitions in which hunters show off the skills of their eagles. More importantly, the festival is a symbol of Kazakh pride and helps preserve their traditions.

　　Sadly, overgrazing has reduced local wildlife populations, meaning there is far less prey to hunt. What's more, many younger Kazakhs are moving to the city to earn a living. However,
25　it is unlikely that the Kazakhs will ever let their traditional lifestyle die. As an old Kazakh proverb explains, "Fast horses and fierce eagles are the wings of the Kazakh people."

WORD FOCUS

⟷ Antonyms for

aggressive

mild
meek
gentle

WORD CHECK

Choose the correct words for the blanks from the highlighted words in the passage.

1. _____ to protect or save sth from damage
2. _____ a series of actions that are carried out in a specific manner
3. _____ relating to a lifestyle of people who move from place to place periodically
4. _____ a short sentence that gives advice about life
5. _____ a group of people of a race or culture that differs from that of the majority

1 What is the passage mainly about?

    a. how hunting has reduced golden eagle populations

    b. why an annual Kazakh festival is no longer held

    c. the different ways golden eagles are used in Asia

    d. the traditional hunting style of the Kazakh people

2 Where would the following sentence best fit in paragraph 2?

> This helps the birds learn to recognize their master's voice.

3 Which is NOT true about eagle hunting?

    a. It requires a series of training procedures to tame the eagles.

    b. It is usually done in winter to get the thickest animal fur.

    c. It was traditionally an important means of getting meat for the nomadic Kazakhs.

    d It is currently a difficult hunting method practiced only by men.

4 Which is NOT mentioned about the Golden Eagle Festival?

    a. the reason that it is held

    b. the approximate number of participants

    c. its economic impact on the Kazakhs

    d. events that it includes

5 According to paragraph 5, why is there far less prey to hunt?

_____

6 Match each topic to the correct paragraph in the passage.

    (1) Paragraph 1 •   • ⓐ the challenges faced by the Kazakhs today

    (2) Paragraph 2 •   • ⓑ when and what the Kazakh people hunt with eagles

    (3) Paragraph 3 •   • ⓒ the traditional hunting style of the Kazakh people

    (4) Paragraph 4 •   • ⓓ how golden eagles are caught and trained to hunt

    (5) Paragraph 5 •   • ⓔ an event that promotes and preserves the eagle-hunting tradition

The Sahara desert, which stretches for more than three million square miles across the northern part of Africa, might seem like a harsh and empty place. But in Tan-Tan, a town in southwestern Morocco, there is a great gathering where the desert comes to life. In May or June each year, thousands of people from more than 30 nomadic tribes attend this festival, called the Tan-Tan Moussem.

The Tan-Tan Moussem was first organized in 1963 as a way for different tribes to socialize and share their local traditions. The gathering was banned for a while in the mid-1970s due to security problems in the region. However, in 2004, thanks to efforts to revive the event, it once again became the largest gathering of nomadic tribes in North Africa.

During the festival, the desert is turned into a temporary city, as hundreds of tents are set up to accommodate the nomadic tribes. Aspects of the traditional lifestyles of the tribes are displayed in some of the tents, such as traditional food and handmade crafts. The Tan-Tan Moussem also features a variety of events, including camel trading and musical performances. The most exciting event of the festival, however, is the *Tbourida*. During this thrilling performance, nomadic warriors ride their horses while holding rifles in the air and shouting terrifying war cries.

Recently, economic changes and advances in technology have made it difficult for the Sahara's nomadic populations to maintain their traditional ways of life. This has prompted concerns that their cultural heritages might disappear. For this reason, the Tan-Tan Moussem plays a **critical** role in ensuring that these tribes' unique traditions are not forgotten.

UNESCO has acknowledged the importance of the Tan-Tan Moussem by adding it to its Intangible Cultural Heritage of Humanity list. This special gathering is now recognized globally as an event that helps the Sahara's nomadic tribes pass down their cultures to future generations.

WORD FOCUS

⊜ Synonyms for

critical

crucial
vital
significant
integral

WORD CHECK

Choose the correct words for the blanks from the highlighted words in the passage.

1. _____ not inhabited by people
2. _____ existing or continuing only for a short period of time
3. _____ to meet people and spend time with them in a friendly way
4. _____ sth that makes sb worry
5. _____ to make sth that has been inactive for a while active again

Scanning

When scanning, we rapidly search for the information we are looking for. The idea behind scanning is to locate specific information without reading through the entire passage. Even if you see a word that you don't understand, keep on going.

MAIN IDEA

1 What is the passage mainly about?

a. the difficulties of living in the Sahara desert

b. an event that preserves the nomadic cultures of the Sahara

c. a serious cultural conflict among nomadic tribes

d. the fascinating history of a town in Morocco

DETAILS

2 Why was the Tan-Tan Moussem banned in the 1970s?

_____

3 The *Tbourida* is an event where _____.

a. nomadic tribes buy and sell traditional food

b. participants trade their camels

c. warriors holding guns ride their horses

d. various traditional crafts are exhibited

4 Which is mentioned as a threat faced by the Sahara's nomadic tribes?

a. Their populations have been rapidly declining in recent years.

b. They are suffering from damage caused by war.

c. Their traditions might be lost due to economic and technological changes.

d. The natural environment of the Sahara desert is getting harsher.

5 Write T if the statement is true or F if it's false.

(1) The Tan-Tan Moussem is held in a Moroccan town once a year.   _____

(2) During the festival, tribes stay in cities outside of the desert.   _____

SUMMARY

6 The sentence below is the first sentence of a short summary of the passage. Choose TWO additional sentences from below to complete the summary.

> Saharan nomadic tribes celebrate their cultures and traditional ways of life at the Tan-Tan Moussem.

a. A major event at the Tan-Tan Moussem is the *Tbourida*, a performance by nomadic warriors.

b. The Tan-Tan Moussem was viewed as a security threat in the 1970s.

c. The Tan-Tan Moussem ensures that nomadic tribes' traditional lifestyles are preserved.

d. The Sahara desert is a difficult place for nomadic tribes to survive.

e. New technologies are used to prevent traditions from being damaged.

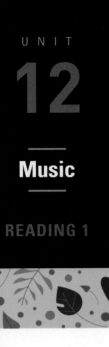

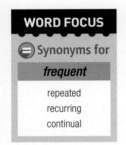

WARM-UP QUESTION • Do you know any natural-born musicians?

In music, sight-reading is the act of playing a piece of music that one has never seen or heard before simply by reading sheet music. While most musicians struggle to do this with fluency, 5 legends exist about the amazing sight-reading abilities of famous composers of the past. These geniuses could sight-read a piece as if they had been playing it for years.

Wolfgang Amadeus Mozart was one such genius. Without any practice or rehearsal, 10 he could look at a sheet of music and play it perfectly on the piano, down to the very last note. This skill came in handy for him when he was writing his own music, as he always knew how each note of a piece would sound before he had even written it down or tried playing it.

Ludwig van Beethoven had a similar ability and is famous for once having played 15 an entire concerto in a new key due to an out-of-tune piano. This is the same as asking (A) an actor, five minutes before a show, to deliver his (B) lines in (C) Swedish instead of English. Like Mozart, Beethoven could mentally "hear" notes without playing them, which became important later in his life when he continued writing music despite going completely deaf.

20 However, most scholars agree that Franz Liszt was likely the most talented sight-reader ever. There is a story about a student composer who brought Liszt a piano concerto he had just written. The music was scrawled messily across several pages, with **frequent** scratch-outs and substitutions. But Liszt took the manuscript from him, glanced at it for a second, and proceeded to play the entire thing—including the orchestra parts— 25 without missing a note! His skill was so great that he is said to have given a perfect performance of every known piece of music in history.

WORD FOCUS

⊜ Synonyms for

frequent

repeated
recurring
continual

WORD CHECK

Choose the correct words for the blanks from the highlighted words in the passage.

1. _____ to write in a careless and untidy manner
2. _____ a character representing a musical tone
3. _____ a writer's original work that has not yet been published
4. _____ the act of replacing one thing with another
5. _____ useful in a variety of ways

Inferring meaning

When reading, you sometimes have to infer meanings. To identify ideas that are not stated directly, you can use common sense or general knowledge. You can also infer meanings based on contexts.

MAIN IDEA

1 What is the passage mainly about?

a. composers with physical handicaps

b. the secrets of reading music quickly

c. unknown composers throughout history

d. musical geniuses with outstanding sight-reading ability

DETAILS

2 In paragraph 3, what are the underlined words (A), (B), and (C) each being compared to?

	(A)	(B)	(C)
a.	Beethoven	key	old notes
b.	Mozart	key	a new concerto
c.	a composer	notes	new music
d.	a musician	music	a new key

3 What was the condition of the manuscript that was brought to Liszt according to paragraph 4?

_____

4 Which of the following is NOT true according to the passage?

a. Not every musician can sight-read a piece of music easily.

b. Mozart could write music easily due to his sight-reading skill.

c. Beethoven's sight-reading ability helped him write music after he went deaf.

d. Liszt often rewrote the messy manuscripts that students brought him.

SUMMARY

5 Use the words in the box to fill in the blanks.

talented   tuned   composers   page   sounded   sheet

Sight-reading

Definition	the ability to play music by reading _____ music you haven't seen before
Example 1 : Mozart	He knew what notes _____ like without having to play them.
Example 2 : Beethoven	He played an entire piece in a different key due to a poorly _____ piano.
Example 3 : Liszt	He might have been the most _____ sight-reader ever because he is said to have performed every known musical work perfectly.

WARM-UP QUESTION • Which style of music is most popular in your country?

These days, when people hear the word "tango," they usually think about the popular and energetic style of dance. But it originally referred to a style of music used to console the sad and the lonely.

5　During the 1880s, thousands of penniless immigrants from Europe came to Argentina, hoping to make their **fortune**s on the plains. However, many failed and gathered in the poorest areas of Buenos Aires. These immigrants felt lost and alone, and they shared their unhappiness through music. They created their own special music and dances, using the rhythms of African slaves and the sounds of Spanish colonists. The sadness of the music was emphasized by the melancholic sounds of a type of 10　accordion known as the bandoneon. From this point onward, tango began to develop.

After World War I, tango became the dominant music style in Argentina. As Argentina's economy gradually developed, tango was refined to make it more fashionable and elegant. The lyrics of the songs slowly moved from the subjects of poverty and the loneliness of immigrants to the general subject of romance. Stars were made: singers, 15　dancers, lyricists, and composers. Carlos Gardel, a famous singer, introduced tango through radio and the movies, which made it a worldwide phenomenon.

However, in 1930, there was a violent change of government in Argentina. People lost their right to vote, along with many other freedoms. ⓐ It was not until the late 1930s that Argentinians got their freedom back. ⓑ They began to enjoy tango—it was once 20　again a part of their daily lives. ⓒ However, tango became less fashionable after the 1940s due to the arrival of American swing and rock and roll. ⓓ From the 1960s to the 1980s, it was enjoyed only by the older generation and by a few enthusiasts.

The current revival dates from the early 1980s, when a stage show called *Tango Argentina* toured the 25　world with a dazzling version of tango. The 1990s became another period of renewal, with tango being influenced by contemporary music like jazz.

WORD FOCUS

◀ Collocations for

fortune

a **huge** fortune
leave a fortune
inherit a fortune

WORD CHECK

Choose the correct words for the blanks from the highlighted words in the passage.

1. _____ graceful in style or form
2. _____ to try to make sb feel better
3. _____ the process of making sth popular again
4. _____ sb who has a lot of passion and interest in sth
5. _____ sb who comes to a foreign country to live there

MAIN IDEA

1 What is the main idea of the passage?

   a. Tango was created by poor immigrants.

   b. Tango had a great impact on swing and rock and roll.

   c. Argentinians like to express their feelings through music.

   d. Tango has developed along with political and social changes.

Identifying time order

Along with dates and times, writers often use related words to show the order of events – for example, *first*, *next*, *then*, *later*, *finally*, and *today*. These words can help you understand a passage better. Read carefully and identify those words.

DETAILS

2 Which is closest in meaning to <u>dominant</u>?

   a. trivial   b. delicate   c. prevailing   d. precious

3 What was Carlos Gardel's contribution to tango according to paragraph 3?

_____

4 Where would the following sentence best fit in paragraph 4?

> A somber mood spread across the country, which left few people interested in singing or dancing.

5 Put the following information about tango in order, according to the passage.

ⓒ → ⓐ → _____ → _____ → _____ → ⓕ

   ⓐ Tango became the most popular Argentine music style and focused on the subject of love.

   ⓑ Unfortunate political changes discouraged people from playing music or dancing.

   ⓒ Immigrants mixed African and Spanish musical styles to create their own music.

   ⓓ A traveling tango show revived the music style both in Argentina and abroad.

   ⓔ Popular American music caused tango to go out of style in Argentina.

   ⓕ With more modern influences, tango became an international sensation.

SUMMARY

6 The sentence below is the first sentence of a short summary of the passage. Choose TWO additional sentences from below to complete the summary.

> Since the late 19th century, tango has undergone several changes.

   a. Economic and social factors affected the style and popularity of tango.

   b. In Argentina, people didn't accept the elegant style of tango.

   c. The introduction of American music had a positive influence on tango.

   d. Tango was created by poor immigrants in Buenos Aires during the 1880s.

   e. In the 1970s, younger generations enjoyed tango more than older ones did.

WORD REVIEW TEST

[1~4] Choose the word that is closest in meaning to the underlined word.

1. He cornered a snake in his yard and managed to <u>capture</u> it.
    a. catch   b. terrify   c. recognize   d. revive

2. The purpose of the United Nations is to <u>maintain</u> world peace.
    a. promote   b. spread   c. ensure   d. keep

3. Luckily, she <u>spotted</u> the mistake before submitting her test.
    a. committed   b. detected   c. ignored   d. displaced

4. David has been <u>banned</u> from driving for a year as a result of drunk driving.
    a. approved   b. examined   c. prohibited   d. trained

[5~8] Connect the matching words in columns A and B.

A		B
5. accommodate •		• a. a festival
6. earn •		• b. traditions
7. attend •		• c. guests
8. preserve •		• d. a living

[9~12] Choose the best word to complete each sentence. (Change the form if needed.)

pass down   harsh   release   show off   stretch   participate in

9. Many species can't survive in this _____ climate.

10. The turtles were rescued and _____ back into the sea.

11. A town once _____ along the beautiful coastline but there's nothing now.

12. He used to _____ his wealth by driving a luxurious car.

[13~16] Choose the correct word for each definition.

acknowledge   aggressive   thrilling   prey   craft   population

13. something made using skills like weaving or carving, especially by hand:

14. an animal that is hunted and eaten by a predator:

15. to recognize the importance or quality of someone or something:

16. behaving in a combative or threatening way:

[1~3] **Choose the word that is closest in meaning to the underlined word.**

1. Don't try to <u>console</u> me. I know it was my fault.
   a. disturb   b. comfort   c. change   d. understand

2. May I copy the <u>entire</u> book?
   a. new   b. valuable   c. whole   d. boring

3. I <u>scrawled</u> her phone number in my address book.
   a. asked   b. remembered   c. searched   d. scribbled

[4~7] **Connect the matching words in columns A and B.**

A		B
4. feel •		• a. the 16th century
5. date from •		• b. lost and alone
6. play •		• c. lines on a stage
7. deliver •		• d. a piano concerto

[8~11] **Choose the best word to complete each sentence.**

8. The numbers at the bottom _____ to the page numbers.
   a. emphasize   b. proceed   c. reflect   d. refer

9. My friend Brenda has suddenly gone _____ in one ear.
   a. blind   b. deaf   c. frequent   d. melancholic

10. He made a _____ through dishonest business practices.
    a. fortune   b. phenomenon   c. renewal   d. subject

11. Daniel tried to _____ his way of speaking.
    a. gather   b. vote   c. refine   d. struggle

[12~14] **Choose the correct word for each definition.**

substitution   glance   tune   composer   revival   rehearsal

12. someone who writes music:

13. a meeting held to practice a performance:

14. to look quickly at something or someone:

Do you have artistic talent and good handwriting? If so, maybe you should consider calligraphy. Literally meaning "beautiful writing," it is the art of writing letters, characters, words and sentences in an elegant and attractive manner.

The key to becoming an expert calligrapher is being able to control the rhythm and movement of your pen strokes when you write. Calligraphy is one of the more difficult art forms, as you only get one chance to write each character or letter. Each work is completed quickly and spontaneously. Most importantly, there is no going back and correcting errors. Once the artist stops writing, the work is finished.

But calligraphy is far more than just a technical skill. Expert calligraphers must also be able to express specific emotions in their work. They do this not just through the meaning of the words they write, but also through their shape and form. Each stroke of the calligrapher's pen must be in harmony with the rest, resulting in a work that can create deep feelings within its viewers.

There are two essential sides to modern calligraphy. _____(A)_____, it can be a pure art form, like painting or sculpting. In this type of calligraphy, the words themselves may or may not be readable—it is their appearance that matters. However, calligraphy can also be used as a visually pleasing way of communicating a **message**. This kind of functional calligraphy can most commonly be found in fancy wedding invitations and greeting cards. Surprisingly, it is used every time we send an email as well. The @ symbol, used in email addresses, is believed to have originated from calligraphy hundreds of years ago.

So why not give calligraphy a try? By writing beautiful letters and characters in harmony with one another, you can create your own works of art that convey a special message to all who view them.

WORD FOCUS

🔊 Collocations for

message

clear *message*
urgent *message*
leave a *message*
deliver a *message*

WORD CHECK

Choose the correct words for the blanks from the highlighted words in the passage.

1. _____ practical and useful
2. _____ certain or particular; not general
3. _____ to begin to exist or happen from somewhere
4. _____ a single movement of sth like a pen or brush
5. _____ elaborate or sophisticated

Active reading

It's a good idea to highlight and underline important parts when you read a passage. This emphasizes the information in your mind and will make reviewing easier. It will also help you concentrate when reading.

MAIN IDEA

1 What is the passage mainly about?

a. the definition and uses of calligraphy

b. the skills needed to become a calligrapher

c. how to develop your own handwriting style

d. the history of calligraphy as an art form

DETAILS

2 What is the key to becoming an expert calligrapher according to paragraph 2?

_____

3 What is the best expression for blank (A)?

a. For example   b. On the one hand

c. By the way   d. As a matter of fact

4 Which usage of calligraphy is different from the others according to the passage?

a.    b.    c.    d.

5 Which of the following is NOT true according to the passage?

a. Calligraphy literally means "beautiful writing."

b. A good calligrapher doesn't express emotions when writing.

c. Calligraphy is often used for fancy written messages.

d. The @ symbol is an example of functional calligraphy.

SUMMARY

6 Use the words in the box to fill in the blanks.

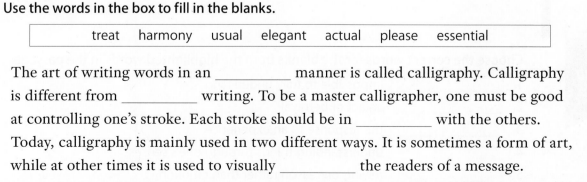

treat	harmony	usual	elegant	actual	please	essential

The art of writing words in an _____ manner is called calligraphy. Calligraphy is different from _____ writing. To be a master calligrapher, one must be good at controlling one's stroke. Each stroke should be in _____ with the others. Today, calligraphy is mainly used in two different ways. It is sometimes a form of art, while at other times it is used to visually _____ the readers of a message.

Surrealist Artist: *René Magritte*

Do you think that a painting should accurately represent reality? If so, the paintings of René Magritte might make you think again. Magritte was a famous Belgian artist who created many interesting surrealist images. His paintings are known for making viewers think about the concept of reality, but doing so with a clever sense of humor.

5 Magritte was part of the surrealism movement, which began partly as a reaction to the horrors of World War I. The artists felt that it was excessive rational thought that had led the world into war. Magritte and the other surrealists focused instead on expressing themselves with creativity and imagination.

Ceci n'est pas une pipe.

Magritte often painted familiar objects, but he 10 placed them in unusual situations, giving new meaning to ordinary things. One of his most famous works, *The Treachery of Images*, is the simple image of a pipe against a plain background. Beneath it, however, Magritte wrote the words "*Ceci n'est pas une pipe.*" 15 This is French for "This is not a pipe." He did this to make the viewer consider the difference between an actual pipe and the image of a pipe.

The Listening Room is similar in that Magritte painted an everyday object—in this case, an apple—in a straightforward way. He challenges our perception, however, by making it 20 appear to be large enough to fill an empty room. Once again, the viewer is left to think about the differences between image and _____(A)_____.

When asked about his artwork, Magritte once said, "When one sees one of my pictures, one asks oneself the simple question, 'What does that mean?' It does not mean 25 anything because mystery means nothing either—it is unknowable." But even if the true meaning of these paintings cannot be known, they still provide art lovers with plenty to think about.

Choose the correct words for the blanks from the highlighted words in the passage.

1. _____ impossible to fully understand
2. _____ an act of betrayal
3. _____ the response to an experience
4. _____ understanding things through one's senses
5. _____ relying on reason rather than emotion

1 What is the passage mainly about?

    a. the personal life of René Magritte

    b. famous artwork of great surrealists

    c. a brief history of the surrealism movement

    d. characteristics of René Magritte's paintings

2 What are Magritte's paintings known for according to paragraph 1?

_____

3 Which is closest in meaning to <u>excessive</u>?

    a. too much   b. quite serious

    c. truly excellent   d. very aggressive

4 Find an appropriate word for blank (A) from paragraph 1.

_____

5 Which of the following is NOT true according to the passage?

    a. Surrealism began as a reaction to the horrors of war to some degree.

    b. The surrealists thought creativity and imagination were important.

    c. Magritte's paintings show everyday objects in familiar settings.

    d. It's not easy for viewers to understand Magritte's paintings clearly.

6 Use the words in the box to fill in the blanks.

unusual	rational	sense	imagination	surrealism	object	perception

René Magritte

- Famous Belgian painter
- Involved in the _____ art movement as a reaction to WWI
  - rejected _____ thinking, focused on creativity and _____
- His paintings
  - *The Treachery of Images*
    - painting of a pipe including the words "This is not a pipe."
    - → the difference between reality and image
  - *The Listening Room*
    - painting of an apple filling up an entire room → challenged _____

WARM-UP QUESTION • Do you know when women earned the right to vote?

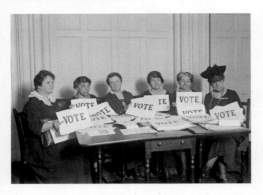

In 1776, when the writers of the Declaration of Independence wrote "We hold these truths to be self-evident, that all men are created equal..." they used the word "men" literally. Women were excluded from many of the rights that were guaranteed in the Declaration of Independence, and in the US Constitution as well. It took women 144 more years to finally receive the basic rights that all human beings deserve.

The first meeting to discuss women's rights was called by Elizabeth Cady Stanton and Lucretia Mott in 1848. At the Seneca Falls Convention, named for the New York town in which it was held, Stanton read the Declaration of Sentiments, a document she wrote based on the Declaration of Independence. It listed the injustices suffered by women in the US and proposed *resolutions to **correct** them.

First on her list of injustices was the fact that women were not allowed to vote, which meant that they had no voice in writing the laws that governed their lives. Also, as married women, their property belonged entirely to their husbands. Women were denied education, entrance into professions, and the right to participate publicly in church affairs.

The resolutions in the declaration demanded that women be recognized as equal to men in all aspects of law and society. It called for women to demand their rights as citizens and to end the practice of allowing men to control their lives and property. Newspapers and religious leaders made fun of the events that took place at the convention and criticized the resolutions. Nevertheless, the convention was the first significant step for the women's rights movement in the US. Finally, women over the age of 21 were given the right to vote in 1920, when the US Constitution was officially changed.

*resolution: an official decision that is made after a group or organization has voted

WORD FOCUS

⊜ Synonyms for

correct

fix
adjust
amend

WORD CHECK

Choose the correct words for the blanks from the highlighted words in the passage.

1. _____ sth that is owned by a person or company
2. _____ to promise that sth will be done
3. _____ to control people through laws
4. _____ the state of being politically free from control by another country
5. _____ to ask for sth in a firm way

1 **What is the passage mainly about?**

    a. the process of creating the US Constitution

    b. the importance of obeying the law

    c. historical changes in gender roles in the US

    d. the beginning of the women's rights movement in the US

2 **Which is closest in meaning to excluded?**

    a. kept out   b. relied on

    c. made up for   d. ended up

3 **What was included in the Declaration of Sentiments according to paragraph 2?**

_____

4 **All of the following describe injustices experienced by women EXCEPT**

    a. being denied the right to vote

    b. not being able to own property if they were married

    c. being restricted from having certain jobs

    d. not being able to attend church

5 **Which is NOT true about the Seneca Falls Convention according to the passage?**

    a. It discussed the improvement of women's basic rights.

    b. It was called by the writers of the Declaration of Independence.

    c. Newspapers and religious leaders ridiculed it.

    d. It contributed to the advancement of women's rights.

6 **Match each topic to the correct paragraph in the passage.**

    (1) Paragraph 1 •   • ⓐ the injustices suffered by women in the US

    (2) Paragraph 2 •   • ⓑ the first women's rights meeting in Seneca Falls

    (3) Paragraph 3 •   • ⓒ the effects of the Declaration of Sentiments on women's rights

    (4) Paragraph 4 •   • ⓓ the exclusion of women's rights from the Declaration of Independence

• What do you think are the basic rights of children?

In 1959, the United Nations agreed on a list of rights for children called the Declaration of the Rights of the Child. The list contains ten items, including the rights to education, protection against exploitation, and relief in all circumstances. However, in spite of the declaration, many children could not enjoy these rights because they were forced to
5 _____(A)_____ under harsh conditions.

Almost 40 years later, in 1998, an Indian human rights activist named Kailash Satyarthi organized the Global March against Child Labor, an **enormous** demonstration against the ongoing problem. At the time, it was estimated that there were still 250 million child laborers worldwide. For example, in the United States, around 230,000 children
10 were illegally working on farms picking fruit and vegetables, and about 45 percent of them had dropped out of school. Similar or worse situations existed in nations around the globe.

The Global March against Child Labor began on January 17, 1998, and took place in 103 countries. Over seven million people participated in the demonstration to
15 demand a change. Some of them marched only in their local areas, and others continued on along with Kailash Satyarthi to Geneva, Switzerland. Here, the International Labor Organization (ILO) was meeting to discuss solutions to the problem of child labor. In June, Satyarthi and the other marchers entered the United Nations Office at Geneva and insisted on resolving the issue with the ILO.

20 The march was a great _____(B)_____ because it drew attention to the problem and pressured the ILO to create effective laws against child labor. The agreement the ILO reached was accepted by nations around the world faster than any other set of labor standards they had published. Although the situation has gradually improved since then, the problem persists. The fight continues because around 152 million child laborers are
25 still being exploited. Today, the Global March against Child Labor exists as an organization rather than an event. As a network of teachers, trade unions, and other groups, it works daily to protect children's rights to freedom and education.

WORD FOCUS

⊜ Synonyms for

enormous

huge
massive
immense

**WORD
CHECK**

Choose the correct words for the blanks from the highlighted words in the passage.

1. _____ to talk about sth with other people
2. _____ to make a guess as to amount or degree
3. _____ continuing or still happening
4. _____ a group of people or organizations that work together as a unit
5. _____ to make official information available to the public

MAIN IDEA

1 **What is the passage mainly about?**

a. organizations that give aid to the poor

b. global statistics on severe working conditions

c. the living conditions of child laborers

d. the fight to end the problem of child labor

Making inferences from the context

To effectively understand a passage, we sometimes need to infer facts that are not mentioned. Some writers leave out important information and expect readers to infer it. So, inferring is sometimes necessary to understand what an author is trying to say.

DETAILS

2 **Which rights included in the Declaration of the Rights of the Child does the writer specify?**

_____

3 **Which is NOT mentioned about the Global March against Child Labor?**

a. who started it

b. why it was organized

c. when it began

d. how many people marched to Geneva

4 **What is the best pair for blanks (A) and (B)?**

	(A)	(B)
a.	study	effort
b.	work	success
c.	leave	shock
d.	participate	failure

5 **Write T if the statement is true or F if it's false.**

(1) The Declaration of the Rights of the Child was adopted in 1959. _____

(2) Since 1998, the number of child laborers has dropped more than 50%. _____

SUMMARY

6 **Use the words in the box to fill in the blanks.**

> awareness   education   insist   fight   standard   local   participated

- child labor statistics in 1998: 250 million children forced into labor
  - not able to enjoy rights to _____ and safety
- the Global March against Child Labor: over seven million people _____
  - brought more _____ to children's rights and led to better labor laws
- child labor statistics today: 152 million children still forced to work
  - continued efforts by the Global March against Child Labor to _____ the problem

WORD REVIEW TEST

[1~5] Choose the word that is closest in meaning to the underlined word.

1. It is said that the deadly disease <u>originated</u> in the Far East.
    a. started   b. reappeared   c. spread   d. endangered

2. The lecturer taught us how to manage money in an effective <u>manner</u>.
    a. action   b. way   c. plan   d. knowledge

3. They went to the top of the skyscraper to <u>view</u> the whole city.
    a. sketch   b. reach   c. see   d. attack

4. The patient had an allergic <u>reaction</u> to the new medicine.
    a. effect   b. symptom   c. disease   d. response

5. The <u>essential</u> difference between us is in our attitude toward life.
    a. excessive   b. fundamental   c. necessary   d. special

[6~8] Connect the matching words in columns A and B.

A		B
6. express •		• a. an empty room
7. create •		• b. emotions
8. fill •		• c. works of art

[9~12] Choose the best word to complete each sentence. (Change the form if needed.)

familiar   fancy   perception   appearance   stroke   unknowable

9. That simple necktie doesn't go with my _____ shirt.

10. Ms. Smith finished painting with a few quick _____ of the brush.

11. Your mood, thoughts, and emotions can affect your _____ of pain.

12. He has great interest in the _____ mysteries of the world.

[13~16] Choose the correct word for each definition.

plenty   specific   horror   plain   harmony   reality

13. the way things actually are:

14. simple and having nothing added:

15. a state in which multiple things exist together well:

16. intense fear:

[1~4] Choose the word that is closest in meaning to the underlined word.

1. The immigrants were <u>denied</u> permission to enter the country.
   a. admitted   b. proposed   c. deserved   d. refused

2. These days, <u>professions</u> are being divided into more specific specialties.
   a. occupations   b. documents   c. affairs   d. executives

3. The two presidents had a meeting to <u>resolve</u> the conflict between the two countries.
   a. set up   b. take off   c. deal with   d. turn down

4. She is a politically <u>significant</u> figure.
   a. obvious   b. important   c. enormous   d. trivial

[5~8] Connect the matching words in columns A and B.

	A		B
5.	participate in •	• a.	the results of the survey
6.	make fun of •	• b.	a volunteer activity
7.	drop out of •	• c.	someone
8.	publish •	• d.	school

[9~12] Choose the best word to complete each sentence. (Change the form if needed.)

estimate   exclude   call for   property   activist   take place

9. The film festival _____ in this city every two years.

10. They are _____ who try to defend the rights of animals.

11. In the past, women were _____ from the field of science.

12. It is _____ that over 370 people were killed in car accidents last year.

[13~16] Choose the correct word for each definition.

convention   criticize   march   effective   exploitation   declaration

13. producing the intended result:

14. to walk in a large group to express support or disapproval of something:

15. to point out the faults of someone or something:

16. the act of getting benefits from someone but giving them little in return:

WORD FOCUS

Collocations for

sign

a **clear** *sign*
a **hopeful** *sign*
detect *signs*

WARM-UP QUESTION • Have you ever seen a comet?

In November 1835, a baby was born while a comet lit up the sky. The baby grew up to be the great writer Mark Twain. In 1909 he said, "I came in with the comet in 1835. It is coming again next year, and I expect to go out with it." And he did! Mark Twain died the day after the comet reappeared in 1910.

The comet was Halley's Comet, one of the most famous objects in our solar system. Astronomers believe that there may be as many as one trillion comets traveling through the universe. But only a few thousand of these have actually been observed.

People have been noticing Halley's Comet since 240 BC. It looks like a star with a glowing tail moving across the sky. For a very long time, many people believed it to be a terrible **sign** of bad luck. But, in 1705, an English astronomer named Edmund G. Halley changed their minds. In his book, he said that comets observed in 1531, 1607 and 1682, were actually one comet making return trips every 76 years. He also predicted that the comet would come again in 1758. Unfortunately, Halley didn't live to see it. But when the comet appeared in 1758, _____(A)_____.

Halley's Comet is a very large ball of frozen dust and gas. We cannot usually see it as it travels across the solar system. However, about every 76 years, it passes near the Sun, the heat of which causes some of the frozen dust and gas to melt and burn away. The burning dust and gas reflect the Sun's light, appearing as the comet's famous tail. This is the only time we can see Halley's Comet move dramatically across the night sky.

WORD CHECK

Choose the correct words for the blanks from the highlighted words in the passage.

1. _____ turned into ice
2. _____ emitting light
3. _____ to return the light that hits an object
4. _____ to say what you think is going to happen
5. _____ a scientist who studies the stars and planets

1 What is the passage mainly about?

   a. a writer who observed a comet in the sky

   b. how comets are formed and die out

   c. the best-known comet visible from Earth

   d. what happens when a comet passes near the Sun

2 It was in 1986 that people were last able to observe Halley's Comet. In what year will the comet again be visible from Earth according to the passage?

   a. 2040   b. 2059   c. 2062   d. 2076

3 What is the best expression for blank (A)?

   a. it was beautiful and people enjoyed seeing it

   b. his theory was proven and the comet was named after him

   c. many people failed to observe it and didn't believe Halley

   d. people were terrified because it was considered a sign of bad luck

4 How does the heat of the Sun affect Halley's Comet according to paragraph 4?

_____

5 Which is NOT true about Halley's Comet according to the passage?

   a. Mark Twain was born in the same year it appeared.

   b. Edmund G. Halley discovered it for the first time.

   c. It consists of frozen dust and gas.

   d. It can be seen from Earth as it passes near the Sun.

6 Choose the proper topic of each paragraph.

(1) Paragraph 1	ⓐ how Mark Twain became a great writer ⓑ the special tie between Mark Twain and Halley's Comet
(2) Paragraph 2	ⓐ the most famous comet known to humans ⓑ the biggest comet in the universe
(3) Paragraph 3	ⓐ Halley's Comet: a sign of bad luck ⓑ the truth about Halley's Comet
(4) Paragraph 4	ⓐ when and how Halley's Comet becomes visible ⓑ why the tail of Halley's Comet is famous

The Planet Saturn

Saturn, the sixth planet from the Sun, is known for its large, distinct rings. These rings were first seen in 1610 by Galileo Galilei, but not very clearly. He wondered if they were just two large moons of the planet. Later, with more developed telescopes, astronomers were able to discern the shape of the rings and eventually discovered that they were made of
5 numerous small pieces of material.

In the 1980s, the two Voyager space probes collected more detailed information about Saturn, and exploration continued from 2004 to 2017 with the Cassini probe. Thanks to the detailed images taken by these spacecraft, we got to see that Saturn is surrounded by thousands of small rings. The collected data revealed information about what Saturn's
10 rings are made of, where they might have come from, and how they change.

Billions and billions of individual bits form the rings of Saturn. Some are the size of a mountain and others are the size of a grain of sand. They are made up mostly of frozen water. When seen through a telescope, the rings look like one large disk. However, there are actually four major ring groups and three smaller groups, all separated by gaps. They all
15 orbit the planet at high speeds.

At first, astronomers thought the rings were as old as the planet and were made from material left over when Saturn formed. ■ But the rings turned out to be made of very pure ice, which suggests they are much younger than the planet. ■ If they were old, they would have collected more dust. ■ It's more likely that asteroids or comets collided with some of
20 Saturn's moons, breaking them into pieces in the distant past. ■ The pieces may have then spread out and formed the rings around Saturn.

Regardless of how the rings formed, scientists agree that they won't last long compared with the lifespan of a planet. Saturn's magnetic field pulls the rings' particles inward, causing them to fall onto the planet like rain. The rings are gradually losing mass
25 and will probably disappear within 300 million years.

1 What is the best title for the passage?

ⓐ The Rings of Saturn: More Than Meets the Eye

ⓑ Mysterious Moons and Rings of Saturn

ⓒ Our Solar System: Home of Beauty and Wonder

ⓓ The Exciting History of Space Missions to Saturn

2 The word revealed in the passage is closest in meaning to

(a) shared   (b) analyzed   (c) concealed   (d) uncovered

3 According to the passage, which of the following is true about Saturn?

(a) It was first discovered by Galileo Galilei.

(b) It was not explored by space probes until 2004.

(c) All the particles of its rings are bigger than mountains.

(d) It is surrounded by seven ring groups.

4 Look at the four squares [■] that indicate where the following sentence could be added to the passage.

Instead, astronomers now think the rings could have been made from broken moons.

Where would the sentence best fit?

5 According to the passage, it is possible that the rings of Saturn

(a) formed simultaneously with the planet

(b) are made from dust

(c) will not exist someday

(d) are not actually moving

6 Directions   Look at the sentence in bold. It is the first sentence of a short summary of the passage. Choose THREE answers to complete the summary. Wrong answer choices use minor ideas from the passage or use information that is not in the passage.

Scientists have been learning about Saturn's rings for hundreds of years.

(a) Modern space probes allow us to study the rings in detail.

(b) The Cassini mission followed the Voyager mission in studying Saturn.

(c) The rings do not appear to move when seen through a telescope.

(d) There are many rings made up of orbiting bits of material.

(e) Objects in space are combined with dust and debris over long periods of time.

(f) Compared to Saturn itself, the rings are younger and have a limited life expectancy.

WORD REVIEW TEST

[1~4] Choose the word that is closest in meaning to the underlined word.

1. The accident had been predicted beforehand.
    a. prevented   b. occurred   c. reappeared   d. foreseen

2. Biofuels are used to light up this city at night.
    a. brighten   b. tour   c. develop   d. separate

3. Olive oil is good for our health in numerous ways.
    a. minor   b. a few   c. a lot of   d. serious

4. It's difficult to discern the difference between identical twins.
    a. collect   b. distinguish   c. investigate   d. disclose

[5~8] Connect the matching words in columns A and B.

A		B
5. reflect •		• a. detailed information
6. reveal •		• b. sunlight
7. orbit •		• c. a rock into pieces
8. break •		• d. the Earth

[9~12] Choose the best word to complete each sentence.

9. The lake is hard to find since it is _____ by dense forest.
    a. proved   b. passed   c. discovered   d. surrounded

10. This submarine is specially designed for deep sea _____.
    a. particle   b. exploration   c. universe   d. material

11. As the climate warms up, the ice caps are _____.
    a. melting   b. forming   c. burning   d. growing

12. The sun suddenly _____ from behind a big cloud.
    a. pulled   b. spread   c. appeared   d. observed

[13~16] Choose the correct word for each definition.

theory   telescope   solar   comet   frozen   gap

13. related to the sun:

14. a space between two things:

15. a bright object with a tail that moves around the sun:

16. a plausible principle to explain a phenomenon, which has not been proven yet:

10분 만에 끝내는 영어 수업 준비!

NE Tutor

Ch 엔이튜터 ➕

NE Tutor는 NE능률이 만든 대한민국 대표 영어 티칭 플랫폼으로
영어 수업에 필요한 모든 콘텐츠와 서비스를 제공합니다.

www.netutor.co.kr

NE Tutor ▼
튜터 Mall
교재 / 수업자료
커리큘럼
스마트 문제뱅크
E-Book
스마트 클래스

— ⬜ ✕

· 전국 영어 학원 선생님들이 뽑은 NE Tutor 서비스 TOP 4! ·

 교재 수업자료 ELT부터 초중고까지 수백여 종 교재의 부가자료, E-Book,
어휘 문제 마법사 등 믿을 수 있는 영어 수업 자료 제공

 커리큘럼 대상별/영역별/수준별 교재 커리큘럼 & 영어 실력에 맞는
교재를 추천하는 레벨테스트 제공

 한국 교육과정 기반의 IBT 영어 테스트 어휘+문법+듣기+독해 영역별 영어
실력을 정확히 측정하여, 전국 단위 객관적 지표 및 내신/수능 대비 약점 처방

 문법 문제뱅크 NE능률이 엄선한 3만 개 문항 기반의 문법 문제 출제 서비스,
최대 50문항까지 간편하게 객관식&주관식 문제 출제

NE_Tutor

NE능률의 모든 교재가 한 곳에 – 엔이 북스

NE_Books

www.nebooks.co.kr ▼

NE능률의 유초등 교재부터 중고생 참고서,
토익·토플 수험서와 일반 영어까지!
PC는 물론 태블릿 PC, 스마트폰으로 언제 어디서나
NE능률의 교재와 다양한 학습 자료를 만나보세요.

✓ 필요한 부가 학습 자료 바로 찾기
✓ 주요 인기 교재들을 한눈에 확인
✓ 나에게 딱 맞는 교재를 찾아주는 스마트 검색
✓ 함께 보면 좋은 교재와 다음 단계 교재 추천
✓ 회원 가입, 교재 후기 작성 등 사이트 활동 시 NE Point 적립

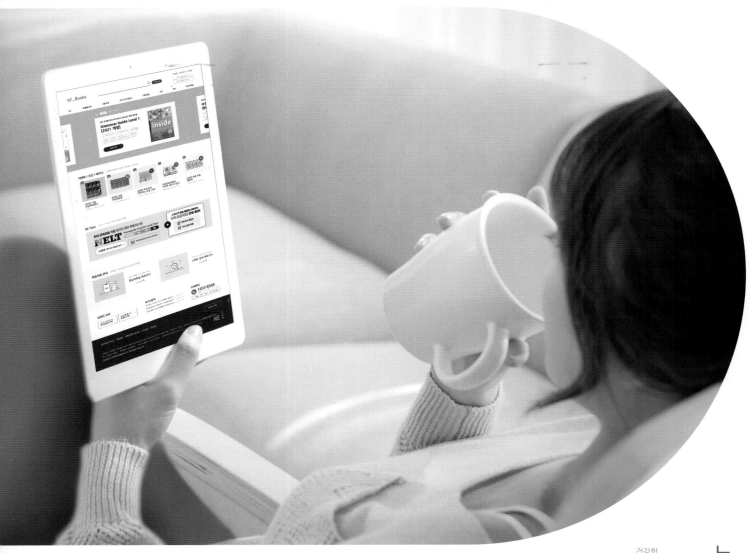

영어교과서 리딩튜터 능률보카 빠른독해 바른독해 수능만만 월등한 개념 수학 유형더블
NE_Build & Grow   NE_Times   NE_Kids(굿잡,상상수프)   NE_능률 주니어랩   아이챌린지

건강한
배움의 즐거움

NE 능률

READING
EXPERT

A 5-LEVEL READING COURSE for EFL Readers

4

NE _ Neungyule

Answers & Explanations

READING EXPERT

A 5-LEVEL READING COURSE for EFL Readers

4

Answers & Explanations

Reading 용어 및 지시문

Ⅰ. 글의 구조와 관련된 용어

- **passage(지문):** 한 주제를 다룬 하나의 짧은 글을 말한다. 여러 개의 단락이 모여 한 지문을 구성한다.
- **paragraph(단락):** 글쓴이가 하나의 주제에 대하여 전개해 나가는 서로 연관된 여러 문장의 집합을 말한다. 흔히 들여쓰기로 단락과 단락 사이를 구분한다.
- **main idea(요지):** 글쓴이가 말하고자 하는 바, 즉 중심이 되는 견해로 보통 문장으로 표현된다.
- **topic sentence(주제문):** 글쓴이의 중심적 견해를 담고 있는 문장으로 각 단락에는 topic sentence가 있다.

Ⅱ. 지시문

- **What is the best title for the passage?** (이 글에 가장 알맞은 제목은?)
- **What is the passage mainly about?** (이 글은 주로 무엇에 관한 내용인가?)
- **What is the main idea of the passage?** (이 글의 중심생각[요지]은 무엇인가?)
- **What is the best word [expression] for blank (A)?** (빈칸 (A)에 들어갈 말로 가장 알맞은 것은?)
- **What is the best pair for blanks (A) and (B)?** (빈칸 (A)와 (B)에 들어갈 말을 짝지은 것 중 가장 적절한 것은?)
- **Which is closest in meaning to appreciated?** (appreciated의 의미와 가장 가까운 것은?)
- **What does the underlined part mean?** (밑줄 친 부분이 의미하는 것은?)
- **What can be inferred from the underlined part?** (밑줄 친 부분에서 유추할 수 있는 것은?)
- **Which of the following is NOT mentioned in the passage?** (다음 중 이 글에서 언급되지 않은 것은?)
- **Which of the following is NOT true according to the passage?** (다음 중 본문의 내용과 일치하지 않는 것은?)
- **Write T if the statement is true or F if it's false.** (진술이 참이면 T, 거짓이면 F를 쓰시오.)
- **Where would the following sentence best fit?** (다음 문장이 들어갈 위치로 가장 알맞은 곳은?)
- **Use the words in the box to fill in the blanks.** (상자 안의 단어를 골라 빈칸을 채우시오.)
- **Match each topic to the correct paragraph in the passage.** (각 주제와 본문의 단락을 알맞게 연결하시오.)

UNIT 01.
Places

READING 1 — p. 8~9

WORD CHECK

1. sphere 2. entire 3. memorable 4. balance
5. demonstrate

▶ mark: to give an indication of sth

정답

1. a 2. His work showed that our planet, once considered to be a perfect sphere, is actually flatter at the poles and bulges at the equator. 3. d 4. b 5. c
6. equator, measurements, sphere, mark, conduct

해석

여기 흥미로운 사실이 있다. 지구 전체를 돌지만, 적도는 단 13개 국가만을 통과한다. 이 국가들 중 하나는 적도를 의미하는 스페인어에서 이름을 땄는데, 바로 에콰도르 공화국이다.

에콰도르는 남미의 북서 해안에 위치해 있고, 북쪽으로는 콜롬비아, 남쪽으로는 페루 사이에 끼어있다. 1736년에 샤를마리 드 라 콩다민이라는 이름의 프랑스 수학자는 현재 에콰도르인 이 지역으로 여행을 떠나 일련의 측정을 했다. 그의 연구는 한때 완벽한 구로 여겨졌던 우리 행성이 사실 극에서는 좀 더 편평하고 적도에서는 볼록하다는 것을 보여줬다.

오늘날 라 콩다민의 연구는 '세상의 중심'이라는 뜻의 미타드 델 문도라는 이름의 공원에 있는 30미터 높이의 탑과 함께 기억된다. 이 공원에는 심지어 그 탑을 지나는 노란색 선이 있는데, 그것이 적도의 위치를 표시해 주는 것으로 전해진다. 하지만 GPS 기술은 실제 적도가 북쪽으로 240미터 지점에 위치해 있음을 보여준다. 이 점에도 불구하고 매년 수천 명의 관광객들이 선 양쪽에 발 하나씩을 놓고 선 채로 서로 사진을 찍는다. 그들은 그 선이 정확한지 아닌지에 신경을 쓰지 않는다. 그저 적도로 온 여행의 즐거운 추억을 원하는 것이다.

지리학적 정확성에 관심이 있는 사람들에게는, 적도 박물관에 가볼 것을 추천한다. 미타드 델 문도에서 차로 겨우 2분 거리에 있는 이 박물관은 GPS 계산이 이곳이 정확히 위도 0도 지점에 위치해 있음을 증명한다고 주장한다. 박물관에서는 안내원들이 특별한 과학 '실험들'을 보여준다. 예를 들어, 물이 바로 배수구로 내려가는 것을 보여주기 위해 개수대 하나가 정확히 적도에 놓여 있다. 물이 원래 그래야 하는 것처럼 왼쪽이나 오른쪽으로 회전하지 않는다! 그리고 방문객들은 못 위에 달걀을 세워 보도록 권유받는다. 안내원들은 이것이 적도에서만 가능하다고 말한다. 이 실험들은 과학적으로 사실이 아니지만, 그것들은 여전히 아주 재미있다!

과학적 사실 여부와 상관없이 적도 방문은 기억에 남을만한 경험이다. 사진을 찍을만한 즐거운 장소가 된다는 점 외에도 적도는 우주를 여행하는 커다란 (거의) 원 형태의 행성에 우리가 살고 있다는 것을 상기시켜 준다!

구문 해설

(5행) ..., a French mathematician [named Charles-Marie
de La Condamine] traveled to the area [that is now

Ecuador] and conducted a series of measurements.

▶ that은 the area를 선행사로 하는 주격 관계대명사

(14행) ..., thousands of visitors each year photograph one

another **standing with** one foot **on** either side of the line.

▶ standing 이하는 동시동작을 나타내는 분사구문
▶ with + 목적어 + 전치사구: ~을 …한 채

(17행) For **those (who are)** interested in geographical accuracy, ...

▶ those who: ~한 사람들

(22행) It doesn't spin to the left or right as it **is supposed to** (**spin** to the left or right)!

▶ be supposed to-v: ~하기로 되어 있다, ~해야 한다

READING 2 — p. 10~11

WORD FOCUS hardship

difficulty 어려움, 곤경 / adversity 역경 / suffering 고통, 고난 / misfortune 불행, 역경

WORD CHECK

1. faraway 2. international 3. civilian 4. equality
5. conflict

▶ educate: to give sb useful information or knowledge so that they can learn it

정답

1. a 2. b 3. It drew international attention to South Africa, which increased the pressure to end apartheid.
4. b 5. (1) F (2) F (3) T 6. (1) ⓒ (2) ⓑ (3) ⓐ (4) ⓔ
(5) ⓓ

해석

남아프리카 공화국 케이프타운의 해안에서 7킬로미터 떨어진 곳에는 로벤섬이라고 불리는 유네스코 세계 문화유산이 있다. 1652년에 네덜란드인들이 남아프리카 공화국에 정착하기 위해 왔을 때 그 섬에 살고 있던 가장 큰 생물체는 물개였다. 실제로 '로벤'이라는 이름은 '물개'를 의미하는 네덜란드어에서 유래되었다. 그러나 이 섬을 가치 있게 만드는 것은 그것의 식민지 시대의 역사이다.

더 많은 식민지 개척자들이 아프리카로 이주함에 따라, 이미 그곳에 살고 있던 사람들과의 갈등이 곳곳에서 생겨났다. 그러므로 네덜란드인들은 자신들에게 대항하는 사람들은 누구든지 투옥할 곳이 필요했고, 그들은 로벤섬을 골랐다. 군인들, 민간인들, 그리고 여러 부족의 지도자들이 그 섬에 투옥되었다. 심지어 멀리 떨어진 식민지에서 네덜란드의 통치에 저항하는 왕과 왕자들도 그곳으로 연행되어 죄수가 되었다.

1800년대에 로벤섬은 또한 중병을 앓는 사람들의 수용소가 되었다. 정신병이 있거나 나병을 앓는 사람들은 다른 사람들로부터 멀리 떼어놓기 위해 그 섬으로 보내졌다. 처음에, 그들 중 일부는 그들이 원하면 떠나도록 허용되었으나 나중에는 강제로 머물러야 했다. 이 관행은 1931년까지 계속되었다.

아파르트헤이트로 알려진 정부가 승인한 인종 차별 제도 하에서, 로벤섬은 인종 평등을 원하는 정치 지도자들을 수감하기 위한 최고 보안 수용소로 사용되었다. 이들 중 가장 유명한 사람은 넬슨 만델라였는데, 그는 1964년부터 1982년까지 18년 동안 그곳에 수감되어 있었다. 넬슨 만델라의 수감은 남아프리카 공화국에 국제적인 관심을 끌어모았으며, 이는 아파르트헤이트를 철폐하기 위한 압력을 강화했다. 로벤섬의 수용소로서의 시기는 아파르트헤이트 정책을 폐지하기 위한 남아프리카 공화국 사람들의 노력 덕분에 1991년에 막을 내렸다. 평등이라는 대의를 위해 고난을 겪은 만델라와 다른 이들로 인해, 로벤섬은 억압을 극복하는 것의 상징이 되었다.

1997년에 로벤섬의 많은 유적지들이 박물관으로 바뀌었다. 그때부터 로벤섬 박물관은 사람들에게 섬의 역사를 교육하기 위해 학교 프로그램과 투어를 운영해오고 있다. 과거의 불평등을 기억함으로써, 사람들은 더 나은 미래를 만들도록 동기를 부여받을 수 있다.

구문 해설

1행 Seven kilometers from the coast of Cape Town, South Africa, is a UNESCO world heritage site [called Robben Island].
▶ 부사구가 강조되어 앞으로 나오면서 주어와 동사가 도치됨

5행 In fact, the name "Robben" **is derived from** the Dutch word [meaning "seal."]
▶ be derived from: ~에서 나오다[파생되다]

9행 Therefore, the Dutch needed a place **to imprison** *whoever* fought against them, ...
▶ to imprison ... them은 a place를 수식하는 형용사적 용법의 to부정사
▶ whoever: ~하는 사람은 누구든지

19행 The most famous of these was Nelson Mandela, **who** was imprisoned there for 18 years, from 1964 to 1982.
▶ 보어가 강조되어 앞으로 나오면서 주어와 동사가 도치됨
▶ who는 Nelson Mandela를 선행사로 하는 계속적 용법의 주격 관계대명사

27행 **By remembering** the injustice of the past, people can *be motivated to create* a better future.
▶ by v-ing: ~함으로써
▶ be motivated to-v: ~하도록 동기부여되다

UNIT 02.
Jobs

READING 1   p. 12~13

WORD CHECK
1. respectively   2. particular   3. expert   4. breathe
5. delicate
▶ pair: to bring together two things that match well

정답
1. a   2. Because the water we drink contains all kinds of different salts and minerals that give it a unique taste.
3. d   4. ⓑ-ⓒ-ⓐ   5. c   6. diners, matches, detects, aroma

해석
'소믈리에'라는 단어를 들으면, 당신은 아마도 와인을 생각할 것이다. 전통적으로 소믈리에는 식사하는 사람들이 자신들의 음식과 잘 어울리는 적절한 와인을 고르도록 도와주는 와인 전문가이다. 하지만 또 다른 종류의 소믈리에도 있는데, 바로 물 전문가이다.

워터 소믈리에는 각기 다른 종류의 물이 어떤 맛을 내는지에 대해 정말 작은 차이도 감지할 수 있다. 당신은 일상생활을 하면서 아마 물의 맛에 대하여 생각하지는 않겠지만, 새로운 곳으로 여행을 간다면 아마 익숙했던 물과는 다른 물맛이 난다는 것을 알아차릴 것이다. 우리가 마시는 물은 고유한 맛을 주는 모든 종류의 각기 다른 염분과 미네랄을 포함하고 있기 때문이다. 이러한 이유로 어떤 고급 식당은 손님이 고를 수 있게 선택 가능한 (다양한) 물들을 제공한다. 워터 소믈리에는 식당이 이러한 목록을 만드는 것을 돕고 어떤 종류의 물이 어떤 음식과 가장 잘 맞을지를 추천한다.

그럼 워터 소믈리에는 어떻게 물맛을 보는 걸까? 우선, 코에 잔을 갖다 대고 희미한 향을 음미하기 위해 깊이 숨을 들이쉰다. 그다음, 소량의 물을 마시고 혀 주위로 물을 움직여보고 삼킨다. 이러한 과정은 소믈리에가 물의 모든 섬세한 맛을 감지할 수 있게 해준다. 물의 맛을 설명하기 위해 'acidity(산성)', 'effervescence(비등)', 'structure(구조)'와 같은 특정한 단어들이 사용된다. 이 단어들 각각은 물의 신선함, 거품, 맛이 얼마나 깊고 복합적인지를 나타낸다.

식당에서는 그들이 제공하는 물에 점점 더 중점을 두고 있다. 예를 들면, 로스앤젤레스의 한 식당에서는 전 세계의 20가지 다른 종류의 물을 제공하고 있다. 가장 비싼 물은 한 병에 20달러나 한다! 그러니 다음에 물을 마시게 되면, 그냥 삼키지 마라. 맛이 어떤지 생각하는 시간을 가져보라!

구문 해설
3행 ... who **help** diners **choose** an appropriate wine to go with their meal.
▶ help + 목적어 + (to)-v: ~가 …하도록 돕다

Water sommeliers can detect the smallest differences in [**how** different types of water taste].

▶ how가 이끄는 절은 전치사 in의 목적어로 쓰인 간접의문문으로 「의문사 + 주어 + 동사」의 어순

11행 ... the water tastes different than the water [(**that** [**which**]) you are used to].

▶ you 앞에 목적격 관계대명사 that[which]이 생략됨

READING 2   p. 14~15

WORD FOCUS   family

family ties 가족의 유대 / family business 가업 / nuclear family 핵가족 / extended family 대가족

WORD CHECK

1. aim   2. eliminate   3. advancement   4. modify
5. primary

▶ adjust: to adapt to a new situation

정답

1. c   2. It is to find new uses for old products that would otherwise be thrown away.   3. c   4. a   5. d
6. new, reduce, seniors, adjusting

해석

우리는 급격히 변화하는 세계 속에서 살고 있다. 그리고 우리 세계가 변하면서 우리의 직업도 바뀌고 있다. 현재 일자리 시장에 영향을 미치고 있는 여러 이슈가 있다. 이는 환경 훼손을 줄이려는 노력, 인구의 노령화, 기술의 급격한 발전을 포함한다. 이러한 점들을 염두에 두고 아직은 생겨나지 않았지만 아마 곧 생기게 될 직업들이 여기 몇 가지가 있다.

아마 웹 디자이너나 패션 디자이너는 들어봤겠지만, 쓰레기 디자이너는 어떤가? 이 직업 이름이 이상하게 들리겠지만 쓰레기 디자이너의 주요 업무는 달리 쓰임이 없다면 버려지게 될 오래된 제품의 새로운 사용법을 찾아내는 것이다. 업사이클링이라고 알려진 이 과정은 매립지로 보내지는 쓰레기의 양을 줄이는 데 도움을 준다. 몇몇 쓰레기 디자이너는 공장에서 만들어지는 쓰레기의 양을 줄이기 위해 제조 과정을 바꾸기도 한다. 시간이 흐르면 그들은 회사가 물건을 제조하는 방법을 완전히 재설계할지도 모른다!

노스탤지스트는 또 다른 새로운 형태의 디자이너이다. 그들은 자신들의 삶에서 가장 행복했던 시절을 떠올리고 싶어 하는 부유한 노인들을 위해 특별한 집을 설계한다. 노인들은 전형적인 현대식 아파트에서 살기보다는, 1970년대 혹은 1980년대의 집처럼 보이는 주거 공간을 갖게 된다. 요즘 사람들은 더 오래 살고 있고, 많은 나라의 인구가 빠른 속도로 고령화되고 있다. 여러 다른 전문가들과 함께 노스탤지스트는 증가하는 노령 인구 집단의 욕구를 충족시키는 것을 목표로 할 것이다.

로봇은 직업을 창출하기보다는 제거할 것으로 예상된다. 하지만 로봇 상담 전문가는 예외이다! 머지않아 운전을 할 수 있고, 요리도 하고, 집을 청소하는 로봇이 존재할 것이다. 로봇 상담 전문가의 역할은 가족들을 만나 그들의 필요에 가장 잘 맞는 로봇을 선택하도록 도와주는 것이 될 것이다. 또한 그들은 가족 구성원들에게 지속적인 고객 서비스를 제공함으로써 그들 삶에 로봇이 있다는 것에 적응하도록 도와줄 것이다. 로봇이 제대로 효과가 없을 경우에는 가족들이 새로운 로봇을 고르게 해줄 수 있다.

물론 미래에 무슨 일이 일어날지는 그 누구도 정확히 알 수 없다. 하지만 오늘날의 친숙한 직업 중 일부가 사라지고 새롭고 특이한 직업으로 교체될 가능성은 크다.

구문 해설

1행 And as our world changes, **so** do our jobs.
            S   V

▶ '~도 그렇다'라는 의미로 so가 절의 맨 앞으로 나오면서 주어와 동사가 도치됨

13행 Over time, they may completely redesign **the way** [companies make things]!

▶ the way 뒤에 관계부사 how가 생략된 형태임 (the way와 how는 둘 중 하나만 사용함)

23행 The role of robot counselors will be **to meet** with families and (**to**) **assist** them in choosing the robots [that best fit their needs].

▶ to meet과 assist는 명사적 용법의 to부정사이며 병렬 관계임

WORD REVIEW TEST

UNIT 01   p. 16

1. d   2. a   3. c   4. b   5. c   6. a   7. c   8. a
9. b   10. c   11. intelligence   12. aisle   13. remind
14. defy   15. practice

UNIT 02   p. 17

1. d   2. b   3. a   4. b   5. b   6. c   7. d   8. a
9. cost   10. familiar   11. disappearing
12. complex   13. faint   14. currently
15. population   16. swallow

UNIT 03.
Language

WORD CHECK

1. local   2. dialect   3. function   4. switch
5. varied
▶ inability: the state of being incapable of doing sth

정답

1. b   2. a   3. b   4. (1) F (2) F (3) O (4) F
5. mistakes, necessary, dialect, communicate

해석

　　나는 에릭 스미스이고 거의 20년간 원어민이 아닌 사람들에게 영어를 가르쳐오고 있다. 내가 지켜본 가장 흔한 문제점은 학생들이 실수하는 것이 두려워서 말하지 않는다는 것이다. 나는 학생들이 표준 영어를 말하지 못하는 것에 '구속당하는' 것을 볼 때마다, "표준 영어를 말하는 것이 정말 그렇게 중요한가?"라고 자문한다.

　　요즘에 영어는 세계적인 의사소통의 도구로 기능한다. 공항을 거쳐 여행할 때, 나는 낯선 사람들 간에 얼마나 많은 대화가 영어로 이루어지고 있는가에 항상 깊은 인상을 받는다. 심지어 대화를 나누는 쌍방의 어느 쪽도 영어가 모국어가 아닌데도 말이다. 한국 항공사 직원이 프랑스 승객의 질문에 영어로 대답하고 있을 수도 있다. 아니면 베트남 남자가 그 지역 음식에 대해서 이야기하기 위해 이집트 여성과 영어를 사용할 수도 있다. 원어민으로서, 나는 가끔 그들이 무슨 말을 하고 있는지 이해하는 데 어려움을 겪기도 하지만, 그들은 대체로 서로 아주 잘 이해하는 것처럼 보인다.

　　더 흥미로운 것은, 일부 국가에서는 영어가 바뀌고 있다는 것이다. 각기 다른 나라의 사람들은 자기 나라의 문화에 적합하게 영어를 변형시킨다. 예를 들어, 말레이시아에서는 사람들이 Manglish라고 부르는 방언을 말하는데, 이는 약간의 중국어와 말레이시아어가 결합된 영어이다. 특히, 'lah'라는 말이 흔히 사용된다. 이것의 용법은 다양하지만, 동사를 명령어로 바꾸는 데 사용되기도 한다. 예를 들어, 영어의 동사 'drink'는 "Drink, lah!"라고 말함으로써 명령이 될 수 있다.

　　위에서 말한 예들은 모두 영어가 어떻게 실용적으로 쓰이고 있는지를 보여주는 증거이다. 내 말을 오해하지는 말기를 바란다. 나도 여전히 학생들이 표준 영어를 읽고 쓰는 법을 배우는 것이 매우 중요하다고 생각한다. 그러나 언어를 말하는 데는 한 가지 방법만 있는 것이 아님을 이해하는 것 또한 중요하다. 특히 주된 목적이 의사소통하는 것일 경우는 말이다. 표준 영어와 실용 영어를 오가며 전환하는 법을 배운 학생들이 세계화된 미래에 성공할 준비가 가장 잘 되어 있을 것이다.

구문 해설

2행 One common problem [I've seen] is students [not
S　　　　　　　　　　　　　V　C
speaking] because ....

12행 ..., I sometimes **have a hard time figuring** out what they're talking about, ...
▶ have a hard time v-ing: ~하는 데 어려움을 겪다
(= have difficulty[trouble] v-ing)

15행 People [in different countries] modify it **to make** it
S　　　　　　　　　　　　　V　　　　　　O(= English)
fit their native culture.
▶ to make 이하는 목적을 나타내는 to부정사의 부사적 용법
▶ make(사역동사) + 목적어 + 동사원형: ~이 …하게 만들다

22행 I still think **it's very important *for students* to learn**
S　V　　　　　　　　　O
how to read and *write* Standard English.
▶ it은 가주어, to learn 이하가 진주어이며, for students는 to부정사의 의미상 주어
▶ how to-v: ~하는 법

WORD FOCUS   difficulty

cause difficulties 어려움을 초래하다 / overcome difficulties 어려움을 극복하다 / major difficulty 큰 어려움 / financial difficulty 재정적 어려움

WORD CHECK

1. effectively   2. injury   3. disorder   4. respond
5. interpret
▶ frustrating: causing anger or annoyance due to an inability to do sth

정답

1. c   2. They have difficulty making grammatically correct sentences.   3. b   4. a, c   5. c
6. communication, damage, grammatically, respond

해석

　　실어증은 의사소통을 매우 어렵게 만드는 언어 장애이다. 이것은 주로 뇌졸중이나 머리 부상으로 인한 뇌 손상에 의해 초래된다. 실어증은 뇌 손상 위치에 따라 나뉘는데, 손상이 가해지는 뇌의 부위에 따라 다른 문제를 야기하기 때문이다. 가장 흔한 두 가지 유형은 브로카 실어증과 베르니케 실어증이다. 다음 예들은 이런 증상을 겪는다는 것이 어떠한 것인지를 생각해보는 데 도움을 줄 것이다.

　　브로카 실어증이 있는 사람은 "Walk dog."와 같은 문장을 말하는 경우가 아주 흔하다. 그런데 이 말은 무슨 뜻인가? 개가 산책하기를 원한다는 말인가? 개를 산책시키자는 말인가? '누가', '무엇을' 하고 있는지에 대해 말해 줄 대명사나 전치사, 접속사가 없기 때문에 이 문장을 해석하는 데는 여러 가지 방법이 있을 수 있다. 브로카 실어증이 있는 사람들은 문법적으로 옳은 문장을 만드는 데 어려움을 겪는다. 이 사람들에게는, 다른 사람들에게 자신을 이해시키는 것이 힘들고 절망적이다.

이와 대조적으로, 베르니케 실어증은 이해력에 문제를 초래한다. 이 증상으로 고통받는 사람들은 말은 쉽게 하지만 다른 사람의 말을 이해하는 데 어려움을 겪는다. 이는 그들의 대화가 말이 안 되는 경우가 종종 있음을 의미한다. 예를 들어, 베르니케 실어증이 있는 사람에게 "점심 먹었어요?" 라고 묻는다고 하자. 그 사람은 "그가 오기를 내가 바란다는 걸 당신도 알잖아요."와 같은 대답을 할 것이다. 짐작할 수 있듯이 이 사람들에게도 대화는 역시 힘들다.

보통 실어증의 치료법으로 언어 치료가 권장된다. 그것은 일부 환자들이 장애를 극복하고 제한된 능력으로 보다 효과적으로 의사소통하는 법을 배우는 데 도움을 준다. 실어증 환자들에게는 또한 다른 사람들의 도움이 필요하다. 가족들은 실어증 환자들이 의사소통이나 정서적, 심리적 문제를 다루는 것을 돕는 데 중요한 역할을 할 수 있다.

구문 해설

[1행] Aphasia is <u>a language disorder</u> [that makes **it** very difficult **to communicate**].

▶ it은 가목적어, to communicate가 진목적어

[8행] ... help you imagine [**what** *it* is like *to suffer* from these conditions].

▶ what이 이끄는 절은 imagine의 목적어로 쓰인 간접의문문이므로 「의문사 + 주어 + 동사」의 어순

▶ it은 가주어, to suffer 이하가 진주어

[19행] ..., conversations are **just as** difficult for these people.

▶ 문장 뒤에 just as와 호응하는 어구 as for people with Broca's aphasia가 생략되어 있음

UNIT 04.
Social Issues

READING 1
p. 22~23

WORD FOCUS unreliable

dependable 믿을 수 있는 / trustworthy 신뢰할 수 있는 / credible 믿을만한 / believable 신용할 수 있는

WORD CHECK

1. possess 2. refuse 3. stereotype 4. resistant
5. racism
▶ promotion: an advancement within an organization

정답

1. c 2. He created it to help bring attention to the social problems older people sometimes face.
3. b 4. b 5. b 6. discrimination, rights, experience, employment, individuals

해석

차별이란 사람들이 가지고 있는 어떤 특징 때문에 그들을 불공평하게 대하는 행동이다. 당신은 인종 차별, 성차별주의에 관하여는 아마 잘 알고 있겠지만, 사람들이 나이 때문에 불평등하게 대우받을 수도 있다는 것은 모를 수도 있다. 이것은 연령차별주의라고 알려져 있다.

'연령차별주의'라는 용어는 노인들의 권리를 보호하는 데 관심이 있었던 미국인 의사이자 작가인 로버트 버틀러에 의해 1969년에 처음 사용되었다. 그는 노인들이 때때로 마주하게 되는 사회문제에 이목을 집중시키고자 그 용어를 만들었다.

자주 우리는 노인을 공경해야 한다고 하지만, 많은 사람들이 그들은 느리고, 기억력이 좋지 않거나, 현대 기술을 사용하는 방법을 배우지 못한다는 고정관념을 믿는다. 또한, 노인들은 창의적이지 않고 변화를 거부하여 결정을 잘 내리지 못하는 사람들로 정형화되어 있기도 하다. 이런 이미지는 특히 노인들이 일터에 있거나 새로운 직업을 구하려고 할 때 상당히 해로울 수 있다.

하지만 노인들만 연령차별주의를 경험하는 것은 아니다. 10대들과 젊은 청년들도 가끔 비슷한 문제를 겪는다. 어떤 회사는 나이가 어린 근로자들의 고용을 거부하거나, 나이가 많은 직원들보다 더 낮은 임금을 지급한다. 무보수 인턴십의 문제도 있다. 그것은 업무 경험을 제공하려고 만들어졌지만, 종종 젊은 구직자들이 무급 인력을 제공하도록 교묘히 조종하여 그들을 이용하는 데 쓰인다.

노인들처럼 젊은 사람들도 특정한 부정적인 고정관념에 대처해야 한다. 관리자가 젊은 사람들은 게으르고 믿을 수 없다는 의견을 가지고 있어서 몇몇은 회사에서 승진하지 못한다. 또 어떤 젊은이들은 집주인이 젊은 사람들은 무책임하고 시끄럽다고 생각해서 아파트 건물에 (입주하지 못하게) 돌려 보내지기도 한다.

요즘 점점 더 많은 사람들이 연령차별주의에 의해 야기되는 문제들을 인지하고 있다. 하지만 이것은 뿌리 뽑기에는 어려운 문제일 수 있다. 나이에 관련된 많은 고정관념들이 사회의 한 부분으로 용인되어 왔다. 하지만 나이가 많든 적든 간에 우리는 모든 사람들을 특별한 개개인으로 대할 것을 명심함으로써 우리의 역할을 다할 수 있다.

구문 해설

[7행] He created it to help bring attention to <u>the social problems</u> [(**that**[**which**]) older people sometimes face].

▶ the social problems 뒤에 목적격 관계대명사 that[which]이 생략됨

[9행] ... we must respect **the elderly**, many of us believe <u>the stereotypes</u> *that* <u>they are slow, have bad</u>

memories, or are unable to learn [**how to use modern technology**].

- ▶ the + 형용사: ～인 사람들 (the elderly = elderly people)
- ▶ that 이하는 the stereotypes와 동격 관계
- ▶ 「how + to-v」는 '～하는 법'의 의미로, learn의 목적어임

(28행) ..., **no matter how** old or **how** young they are.

- ▶ no matter how: 아무리 ～일지라도 (= however)

READING 2
p. 24~25

WORD FOCUS   cause

cause concern 걱정을 불러일으키다 / cause chaos 혼란을 초래하다 / cause disease 병을 야기하다 / cause damage 해를 끼치다

WORD CHECK

1. currently   2. thrive   3. chronic   4. corporate
5. adverse

▶ evolve: to gradually develop and improve

정답

1. c   2. d   3. d   4. We can encourage them to pass strict laws banning cruelty to animals.   5. a
6. profits, antibiotics, pollute, standards

해석

　농장의 전통적인 모습은 동물을 잘 돌보는 농부가 운영하는 도시 외곽의 한적한 곳이다. 하지만 실제로는 세계의 농장 동물 중 약 3분의 2가량이 현재 공장식 농장에서 길러지고 있다. 그리고 이러한 공장식 농장은 농촌 생활의 평화로운 모습과는 아주 다르다.

　공장식 농장은 동물의 건강과 안전보다 기업의 이윤을 먼저 생각하는 규모가 크고, 복잡한 장소이다. 이 동물들은 빽빽이 한데 모여 거의 움직일 수도 없고, 실내에서 평생을 보내야 하는 경우가 다반사이다. 동물들을 더 빨리 자라게 하기 위해, 공장식 농장에서는 동물들에게 성장 호르몬을 투여한다. 이러한 부자연스러운 성장은 만성 통증과 심장 질병 등 동물의 몸에 많은 문제를 야기한다. 이 동물들이 너무 아플 때에는 치료조차 받지 못한다. 대신 비용을 절감하기 위해 도살을 당할 뿐이다.

　게다가, 공장식 농장은 환경에 피해를 주고 사람들의 건강에 악영향을 끼친다. 한 장소에 그렇게 많은 동물을 두는 것은 많은 양의 쓰레기가 배출된다는 것을 의미한다. 이 쓰레기는 주변 지역의 공기, 땅, 물을 오염시킬 수 있다. 또한, 공장식 농장은 운영에 많은 양의 물과 에너지를 필요로 한다. 공장식 농장은 소비자들에게 위협이 될 수도 있다. 살모넬라와 같은 박테리아는 비위생적인 환경에서 잘 자랄 수 있어 공장식 농장에서 생산되는 육류, 우유, 달걀을 오염시킨다. 그런 박테리아를 없애기 위해 동물들은 많은 양의 항생제를 투여받게 되는데, 이것은 더 큰 문제를 일으킨다. 박테리아는 그야말로 진화하고 더 강해지면서 인간에게 심각한 건강상의 위험을 준다.

　그럼 우리가 어떻게 이 해로운 공장식 농장의 관행을 없애도록 도울 수 있을까? 일단 까다로운 동물 복지 및 환경 기준을 충족하는 농장에서 생산된 육류 및 유제품만 구매하는 것으로 시작할 수 있다. 이런 제품들은 일반적으로 '동물 복지 인증'과 같이 특별한 라벨로 표시되어 있다. 우리는 또한 정치인들이 동물 학대를 금지하는 엄격한 법을 통과시키도록 촉구할 수도 있다. 비록 공장식 농장을 완전히 없애는 것이 불가능할지도 모르지만, 이러한 노력들이 농장에서 동물들을 더 잘 다룰 수 있도록 반드시 도울 것이다.

구문 해설

(1행) The traditional image of a farm is a quiet place in the countryside {**run** by a farmer [*who* takes good care of his or her animals]}.

- ▶ run 이하는 a quiet place in the countryside를 수식하는 과거분사구
- ▶ who는 a farmer를 선행사로 하는 주격 관계대명사

(8행) These animals are packed together so tightly that they can barely move, ...

- ▶ so ～ that + 주어 + can: 너무 ～해서 …하다

(17행) Bacteria ... can thrive in unsanitary conditions, **contaminating** the meat, milk, and eggs [that come from factory farms].

- ▶ contaminating 이하는 연속동작을 나타내는 분사구문

(25행) We can also **encourage** politicians **to pass** strict laws [banning cruelty to animals].

- ▶ encourage + 목적어 + to-v: ～가 …하도록 권장[장려]하다

WORD REVIEW TEST

UNIT 03
p. 26

1. a   2. b   3. c   4. b   5. a   6. d   7. c   8. c
9. a   10. therapy   11. classify   12. recommend
13. comprehension   14. command   15. desire

UNIT 04
p. 27

1. d   2. b   3. c   4. c   5. a   6. b   7. c   8. d
9. a   10. opinion   11. resistant   12. discrimination
13. antibiotics   14. cruelty   15. manipulate

READING 1	p. 28~29

WORD FOCUS separation

division 분할 / disunion 분열 / split-up 분리, 해체

WORD CHECK

1. invasion   2. treaty   3. rebel   4. elect
5. designate

▶ restriction: a rule or law that limits or regulates what people can do

정답

1. a   2. (1) T (2) F (3) F   3. They promised to separate from the UK if they were elected.   4. b   5. ⓐ-ⓒ-ⓑ
6. b, d, f

해석

아일랜드섬과 아일랜드 국가가 같지 않다는 것을 알고 있었는가? 그 섬의 일부는 북아일랜드로 불리며 영국에 속한다. 사실, 120년 동안 그 섬 전체는 영국의 지배를 받았다. 이 일은 어떻게 일어났으며, 아일랜드는 어떻게 자치 국가가 되었을까?

1100년대의 수차례의 침략 이후로 영국은 아일랜드에 어느 정도 정치적 영향력이 있었다. 처음에는 두 국가 모두 가톨릭교였지만, 1500년대에 잉글랜드의 헨리 8세가 개신교를 국교로 채택했고, 이는 아일랜드에도 적용되었다. 그 변화에 불만을 가진 아일랜드 지도자들은 잉글랜드에 대항했다. 잉글랜드 통치자들은 개신교로 바꾸기를 거부한 아일랜드인들의 정치적 그리고 경제적 활동을 제한했다. 게다가 개신교도들을 아일랜드로 이주하도록 장려했고 그들에게 아일랜드 지주들로부터 빼앗은 땅을 주었다.

1800년대에 영국인들은 아일랜드가 연합 왕국에 합류하기로 합의하면 가톨릭교도들의 공직 진출을 금지했던 제한을 없애기로 하는 법안을 도입했다. 그 법령은 1801년 1월 1일에 공인되었으나, 가톨릭교도들에 대한 차별은 계속되었다. 부당한 대우에 지친 많은 아일랜드 사람들이 영국으로부터의 완전한 독립을 원했다. 마침내 1916년에 한 작은 집단이 아일랜드 공화국을 세우기 위해 영국인들에게 대항하는 반란을 일으켰다. 그들은 빠르게 패배했지만, 그들이 일으킨 운동은 그렇지 않았다.

많은 아일랜드 정치인들이 자신들이 당선되면 영국에서 독립하겠다고 공약했고, 1918년에 그들의 당이 선출되어 권력을 갖게 되었다. 그들은 아일랜드 공화국군(IRA)이라고 불리는 집단을 지원했다. 1년 후 IRA는 영국에 대항하는 또 다른 반란을 일으켰다. 2년간의 전쟁 후 1921년에 두 나라는 평화 조약에 서명했다. 북쪽의 개신교도들은 영국을 떠나고 싶어 하지 않았고 그 결과로 북아일랜드가 만들어졌다. 아일랜드의 나머지는 독립을 향한 여정을 시작했다.

1949년까지 복잡한 상황이 지속되었고, 그때 아일랜드 공화국 법령이 마침내 아일랜드와 영국 사이의 모든 정치적 관계를 단절시켰다. 갈등이 몇 해 동안 계속해서 있었지만, 지금은 아일랜드와 북아일랜드 모두 평화와 안정의 시대를 누리고 있다.

구문 해설

(10행) **(Being) Unhappy** with the change, the Irish leaders rebelled against England.
▶ Unhappy ... change는 원인을 나타내는 분사구문으로 앞에 Being이 생략됨

(12행) Furthermore, they **encouraged** Protestants **to move** to Ireland and gave them land [*confiscated* from Irish owners].
▶ encourage + 목적어 + to-v: ~이 …하도록 권장하다
▶ confiscated 이하는 land를 수식하는 과거분사구

(19행) They were quickly defeated, but the movement [(**that**) they started] was not (*quickly defeated*).
▶ they 앞에 the movement를 선행사로 하는 목적격 관계대명사가 생략됨
▶ 반복을 피하기 위해 was not 뒤에 quickly defeated가 생략됨

READING 2 TOEFL	p. 30~31

정답

1. ⓑ   2. ⓓ   3. ⓓ   4. the second square
5. ⓐ, ⓔ, ⓕ

해석

차 조례

영국 식민지 시대에 영국 국회는 미국 식민지에 많은 세금을 부과했다. 식민지들은 영국 국회에 선출된 대표가 없었는데, 이는 식민지 주민들이 영국 시민처럼 대우받지 못했음을 의미했다. 많은 미국인들은 어떤 정치적 권리도 없는 사람들에게 세금을 부과하는 것은 불법이라고 생각했다. 상황은 1773년 차 조례의 통과로 훨씬 더 악화되었다. 이 사건은 미국 독립 혁명의 기폭제가 되었다.

국회의원들은 차 조례가 식민지 주민들을 얼마나 분노하게 할지 알지 못했다. 차 조례의 목적은 동인도 회사가 50만 파운드의 차를 면세로 미국 식민지에 수출하도록 허용하여 그 회사를 돕는 것이었다. 그러나 식민지 주민들은 영국 회사가 차 독점권을 갖는다는 방안이 마음에 들지 않았기 때문에 네덜란드에서 밀수입한 차를 사들여오고 있었다. 보다 싼 가격과 관계없이 식민지 주민들은 국회의 차 조례에 격렬하게 저항했다.

저항의 한 가지 형태로 식민지 주민들은 차 불매 운동을 하기로 했다. 일부 식민지 항구에서는 영국 동인도 회사의 차를 실은 배의 정박을 금했다. 배가 보스턴에 정박하게 되었을 때 애국지사들은 차를 내리지 못하게

할 방도를 생각해내기를 원했다. 자유의 아들들이라는 이름의 한 애국 단체 단원들은 모여서 영국에 분명한 메시지를 전달하기 위해 어떤 행동을 취해야 할지를 정했다.

1773년 12월 16일 밤에, 자유의 아들들의 일부 단원이 미국 원주민 부족의 하나인 모호크족 복장을 하고 배에 올랐다. 그들은 342개의 차 상자를 보스턴 항에 버렸다. 식민지 주민들은 더 이상 가만히 앉아서 자신들의 권리가 무시당하는 걸 보고 있지 않겠다는 것을 보여 주었던 것이다.

영국의 대응은 '불용의 법령'으로 알려진 일련의 법 조항을 통과시키는 것이었다. 이 법 조항의 하나가 보스턴 항을 폐쇄하는 것이었다. 미국인들은 그들이 없앤 찻값을 지불하는 대로 보스턴 항이 바로 재개될 것이라는 통보를 받았다. 그들은 이 법에 분노했고 이제 맞서 싸워야 할 때라고 판단했다. 집회가 소집되었고 1차 대륙 회의가 구성되었다. 혁명이 막 시작되려 하고 있었다.

구문 해설

[2행] The colonies had no elected representatives in British Parliament, **which** meant the colonists weren't treated like British citizens.
▶ which는 앞 절 전체를 선행사로 하는 계속적 용법의 관계대명사

[10행] ... because they didn't like the idea **of** *a British company* **having** a monopoly on tea.
▶ of는 '~라는'의 의미로 쓰여 동격을 나타냄
▶ a British company는 동명사 having의 의미상 주어임

[13행] Some colonial ports **stopped** ships [carrying British East India Company tea] **from docking**.
▶ stop + 목적어 + from v-ing: ~이 …하는 것을 막다

UNIT 06.
IT

READING 1
p. 32~33

WORD FOCUS comfortable

troubled 불안한 / uneasy 편하지 않은 / unpleasant 불쾌한, 불편한 / awkward 어색한

WORD CHECK

1. replace   2. open up   3. assistance   4. empathy
5. virtual
▶ judge: to form an opinion about sb or sth

정답

1. a   2. d   3. d   4. It was designed to help gather behavioral evidence from patients who are suffering from depression or post-traumatic stress disorder.
5. c   6. frustration, negative, suggestions, behavioral, transfers

해석

최근 인공지능(AI) 기술의 빠른 발달 덕분에, AI는 이제 정신 건강 도움과 치료를 제공하기 위해 성공적으로 이용되고 있다. AI가 모든 연령의 환자들을 위해 사용될 수 있는 많은 방법이 있다. 몇 가지 예를 살펴보자.

마일로는 실제 인간처럼 생기고 행동하는 로봇이다. 그것은 자폐증이 있는 아이들에게 도움을 주기 위해 고안되었다. 마일로는 그들이 다른 사람의 감정을 이해하고, 공감을 표현하고, 그들의 사회적 기술이 발달하도록 도와준다. 마일로와 상호 작용을 함으로써 그들은 실제 사회적 상황에서 더욱 자신감을 가질 수 있다. 무엇보다도, 이 로봇 치료사는 똑같은 일을 몇 번을 반복하든 절대 불만을 표현하지 않는다!

컴퓨터와 모바일 기기에서 작동하는 챗봇 치료사인 워봇이 또 다른 예다. 그것은 무엇이 사람들에게 부정적인 사고를 유발하는지 인식하고 그러한 생각을 통제할 수 있도록 도움을 준다. 매일 워봇은 사용자들에게 메시지를 보낸다. 그것은 "오늘 기분은 어때요?"와 같은 단순한 질문을 한다. 워봇 이면의 AI는 그것이 사용자의 응답을 기억하고 기분 변화를 인지하게 해준다. 워봇은 마치 실제 치료사처럼 제안을 할 수 있다. 게다가 사용자들은 그것이 그저 애플리케이션이므로 자신을 절대로 판단하지 않을 것을 알기 때문에 편안함을 느낄 수 있다.

유사하게 엘리라고 불리는 가상 치료사는 우울증이나 외상 후 스트레스 장애를 앓고 있는 환자들로부터 행동 징후를 수집하는 것을 돕기 위해 고안되었다. 워봇처럼 엘리는 전혀 비판을 하지 않아서, 사람들은 쉽게 마음을 열고 민감한 정보를 그것과 공유할 수 있다. 환자가 엘리와 소통을 하는 동안 그것은 그들의 표정, 손짓, 그리고 목소리 톤과 같은 것들을 분석한다. 그다음, 이 데이터는 추가적인 치료 및 요법을 권하는 데 그것을 이용하는 인간 의사에게 전송된다.

AI가 인간 치료사를 완전히 대신할 수는 없지만, 그것은 환자의 데이터를 수집하고 분석하는 데 있어서 의사들에게 큰 도움이 된다. 또한 다른 사람들과 사회적으로 소통하는 데 어려움을 겪는 환자들은 AI에 의해 제공되는 치료가 도움이 될 수 있다. 인공 지능 기술이 계속해서 발달함에 따라 AI 치료는 점점 더 보편화될 것 같다.

구문 해설

[3행] There are many ways [**in which** AI can be used for patients of all ages].
▶ in which는 many ways를 선행사로 하는 「전치사 + 목적격 관계대명사」

[8행] ..., this robot therapist never expresses frustration, **no matter how** many times it repeats the same task!
▶ no matter how: 아무리 ~일지라도 (= however)

<table>
<tr><td>17행</td><td>In addition, users can feel more comfortable **knowing** that it will never judge them, ...</td></tr>
</table>

▶ knowing 이하는 원인을 나타내는 분사구문

<table>
<tr><td>25행</td><td>..., it is a great help to doctors **when it comes to** *collecting* and *analyzing* patient data.</td></tr>
</table>

▶ when it comes to: ~에 관해서라면
▶ collecting과 analyzing은 전치사 to의 목적어로 쓰인 동명사로 이 둘은 병렬 관계임

READING 2   p. 34~35

WORD FOCUS   predict

forecast 예측하다 / anticipate 예상하다 / foresee 예견하다

WORD CHECK

1. personalized   2. utilize   3. concern   4. trend
5. misleading
▶ storage: space that is used for keeping or collecting data

정답

1. d   2. c   3. a   4. Because data is often sold to third parties without the customers knowing.   5. d
6. analyze, purchase, recommendations, privacy, unrelated

해석

한 중학생이 새 청바지 한 벌을 사고 싶어 온라인상에서 가격을 비교해오고 있었다. 놀랍게도 그녀는 방문했던 웹사이트 중 한 곳으로부터 청바지 특별 할인을 광고하는 이메일을 받게 된다. 그녀는 인터넷을 검색하면서 이내 같은 웹사이트의 배너 광고를 보게 된다. 어떻게 이럴 수 있는 것일까? 바로 '빅 데이터'라는 것 때문인데, 이는 고객의 자료가 수집되고 활용되는 방법에서의 혁명이다.

요즘은 기업들이 거대한 양의 고객 자료를 수집하는 것이 어렵지 않다. 어려운 것은 그것을 잘 활용하는 것이다. 적절하게 분석되면 빅 데이터는 구매자가 무엇에 관심을 가질지를 예측하는 데 유용한 유형과 추세를 보여줄 수 있다. 다시 말해, 빅 데이터는 저장 용량의 큰 증가라기보다, 실제로 이 모든 자료를 유용하게 해주는 통계에 근거하고 계산을 요구하는 발전된 방법에 관한 것이다.

기업이 빅 데이터를 가장 잘 활용하는 한 가지 예는 Amazon.com이다. Amazon은 사람들이 웹사이트에서 어떤 물건을 구입하는지, 어떤 물건이 구매자의 가상 쇼핑 카트에 담겨 있는지, 심지어 그들이 보기만 했던 상품들조차 파악한다. 그다음, 고객들에게 개인 맞춤형 쇼핑 경험을 제공하기 위해 이 자료를 활용한다. 구매자들은 그 웹사이트로 돌아오자마자 그들이 이미 구입하려고 했던 상품과 고객이 관심을 가질 것이라고 Amazon에서 예측한 상품을 보게 된다. 사실 현재 Amazon 판매량의 29%가 이러한 추천으로 발생한다.

하지만 자료가 수집되는 고객들과 그것을 사용하려는 기업 모두에게 빅 데이터에 관한 우려가 존재한다. 가장 큰 문제 중 하나는 개인정보로, 고객들이 인지하지 못한 채 제 3자에게 자료가 종종 팔리기 때문이다. 또한 Amazon과 같은 기업들은 인터넷 검색어에 의존하는데, 사람들이 검색하는 단어들이 항상 그들이 사고 싶어 하는 것은 아니기 때문에, 이는 잘못된 판단으로 이어질 소지가 있다. 이러한 문제점들에도 불구하고 빅 데이터가 개인이 온라인 세계와 상호작용하는 방법에 혁신을 일으켰다는 것은 분명하다.

구문 해설

<table>
<tr><td>2행</td><td>**To her surprise**, she receives an email [*advertising* a special sale on jeans ...].</td></tr>
</table>

▶ to one's surprise: 놀랍게도
▶ advertising 이하는 an email을 수식하는 현재분사구

<table>
<tr><td>10행</td><td>**What's** difficult is *putting* it all *to good use*.</td></tr>
</table>

▶ what은 선행사를 포함한 관계대명사
▶ put ~ to (good) use: ~을 (잘) 활용하다

<table>
<tr><td>19행</td><td>..., they are shown both items [**that** they have already considered purchasing] and items [**that** Amazon predicts *that* they will be interested in].</td></tr>
</table>

▶ 첫 번째 that과 두 번째 that은 각각 items를 선행사로 하는 목적격 관계대명사이고, 세 번째 that은 predicts의 목적절을 이끄는 접속사임

WORD REVIEW TEST

UNIT 05   p. 36

1. d   2. b   3. c   4. c   5. a   6. d   7. b   8. d
9. c   10. b   11. b   12. exist   13. act   14. boycott

UNIT 06   p. 37

1. d   2. a   3. c   4. d   5. b   6. d   7. a   8. c
9. replaced   10. privacy   11. capacity
12. analyzing   13. artificial   14. pattern
15. judgmental   16. revolutionize

UNIT 07.
Psychology

READING 1   p. 38~39

WORD FOCUS   flaw

weakness 약점 / defect 결함 / fault 단점, 결점 /
imperfection 불완전, 결함

WORD CHECK

1. competent   2. threat   3. consequence
4. imposter   5. widespread

▶ overwhelming: influencing sb too much to behave or think normally

정답

1. a   2. People with this syndrome have difficulty sharing their ideas or pursuing challenging goals.   3. c
4. ⓒ   5. c   6. talented, unworthy, perfectionists, openly, success

해석

당신은 성공을 누릴 자격이 없는 것 같은 느낌이 드는가? 만약 그렇다면, 당신은 가면 증후군을 겪고 있을 수도 있다. 그것은 당신이 실제로는 다른 사람들이 생각하는 것만큼 유능하지 않다는 확고한 생각이다. 대신에 당신은 사기꾼처럼 느껴질 뿐이다. 그것은 드문 생각이 아닌데, 알베르트 아인슈타인조차 그의 성과가 과분한 관심을 받고 있다고 걱정했다. 그러나, 그것은 부정적인 결과로 이어질 수 있다. 이 증후군을 겪는 사람들은 그들의 생각을 공유하거나 도전적인 목표를 추구하는 데 어려움을 겪는다.

가면 증후군은 1970년대에 폴린 클랜스와 수잔 임스라는 심리학자들에 의해 처음 주목받았다. 그들은 자신들의 여학생들 중 다수가 자신의 학교에 등록할 자격이 없다고 느낀다는 것을 발견했다. 높은 성취를 이룬 여성들만이 이 증후군의 영향을 받는다는 가설을 바탕으로 그들은 더 많은 연구를 수행했다. 그들은 그것이 연령, 인종, 성별과 상관없이 일어나는 널리 퍼진 문제라는 것을 깨달았다.

가면 증후군에는 한 가지 원인이 있는 것이 아니다. 그러나, 그것을 겪는 많은 사람들이 같은 성향을 가지는데, 바로 완벽주의. 그들의 마음에는 결점이 없는 사람만이 성공을 누릴 자격이 있다. 사실 자신의 결점에 집중하는 것은 자연스러운 일인데, 인간의 뇌가 위협 요소로 간주하는 부정적인 것들에 더 깊은 주의를 기울이도록 만들어졌기 때문이다.

가면 증후군에 대처하는 가장 좋은 방법은 그저 이야기하는 것이다. 그것을 겪는 사람들은 대개 다른 사람들에게 자신들의 성과에 관해 묻는 것을 두려워한다. 그들은 자신이 실제로는 사기꾼이라는 것을 그들(다른 사람들)이 알게 될까 봐 걱정한다. 그러나 실제로는 정 반대가 사실이다. 그들이 마음을 열고 자신들의 두려움과 의혹에 관해 상의할 때, 자신이 정말로 성공을 누릴 자격이 있다는 것을 깨달을 가능성이 있다. 게다가, 그들은 사기꾼

처럼 느끼는 것은 자신뿐만이 아니라는 것을 알게 될 것이다.

가면 증후군을 영영 사라지게 만들 방법은 없다. 그렇지만, 터놓고 솔직하게 소통하는 것은 부정적인 생각을 통제하고 그것들이 감당할 수 없게 되는 것을 예방할 수 있다.

구문 해설

3행 It's a strong feeling **that** you aren't really *as competent as* others think you are.
- ▶ that이 이끄는 절은 a strong feeling과 동격 관계
- ▶ as + 형용사/부사의 원급 + as ~: ~만큼 …한[하게]

11행 They found {**that** many of their female students felt [(*that*) they didn't deserve to be enrolled at their college]}.
- ▶ 첫 번째 that 이하는 동사 found의 목적어 역할
- ▶ felt 뒤에 목적절을 이끄는 접속사 that이 생략됨

18행 ... the human brain is hardwired to pay closer attention to negative things, **which** it *considers* a threat.
- ▶ which는 negative things를 선행사로 하는 계속적 용법의 관계대명사
- ▶ consider A B: A를 B라고 여기다[생각하다] (A = negative things)

25행 There is no way **to *make*** the imposter syndrome *go* away forever.
- ▶ to make는 way를 수식하는 형용사적 용법의 to부정사
- ▶ make(사역동사) + 목적어 + 동사원형: ~을 …하게 만들다

READING 2   p. 40~41

WORD FOCUS   impression

overall impression 전반적인 인상 / initial impression 첫인상 / give an impression 인상을 주다 / get an impression 인상을 받다

WORD CHECK

1. overshadow   2. promote   3. revolutionary
4. psychological   5. sophisticated

▶ tactic: specific method or strategy used to accomplish a goal

정답

1. d   2. It is the strong impression left on a consumer by the first information that he or she receives about a certain product.   3. b   4. d   5. (1) F (2) T (3) F
6. psychological, first, recently, influence, research

많은 사람들은 자신이 스스로 구매 결정을 내린다고 생각한다. 하지만 사실은 제품에 관한 의견에 영향을 주는 여러 가지 심리적 요인이 있다. 이 요인들 중 가장 영향력이 큰 두 가지는 '초두성 효과'와 '최신 효과'라고 불리는 것들이다.

초두성 효과는 어떤 제품에 관해서 소비자가 받은 첫 번째 정보에 의해 만들어진 강력한 인상이다. 광고에서 흥미롭고 혁신적이라고 보여주는 한 제품을 처음 봤다고 가정해보라. 이 정보는 뒤이어 나오는 정보보다 머릿속에 더 오래 남을 가능성이 있다.

하지만 최신 효과는 훨씬 더 강력하다고 여겨진다. 이것은 상품에 관해 마지막으로 받은 정보에 의해 만들어진 인상이다. 따라서 긍정적인 첫인상을 가진 뒤에 부정적인 평가를 듣게 되면 최신 효과가 커지게 되고, (제품에 대한) 느낌도 부정적으로 변하게 된다. 영향력이 큰 이 두 가지 효과가 당신이 첫인상과 마지막 인상 사이에서 얻게 된 것을 무색하게 만든다. 그 결과 다량의 정보가 당신이 형성하는 의견에 거의 영향을 미치지 않게 된다.

마케팅 담당자들은 이것에 관해 아주 잘 알고 있다. 좋은 첫인상을 보장하기 위해서 그들은 부정적으로 평가될 가능성이 있기 전에 인쇄물, 라디오, 텔레비전 및 인터넷 광고를 통해 제품을 홍보하려고 노력한다. 또한 제품이 세련되고 매력적으로 보이도록 포장을 디자인하면서 최신 효과를 통제하려고 한다. 그들은 이 마지막의 긍정적인 느낌이 소비자가 가지고 있을 수 있는 이전의 부정적인 의견을 모두 지우기를 바란다.

이것은 어떤 제품에 관해 당신이 조사하는 많은 것이 결국에는 마케팅에 의해 지워진다는 것을 의미한다. 그럼 당신은 무엇을 할 수 있을까? 가지고 싶은 물건이 있다면 어떤 광고도 보지 않고 소비자 평가와 같은 신뢰할 수 있는 자료를 찾아보라. 이것은 광고 전략에 통제를 받기 전에 당신이 지식에 근거한 의견을 갖추도록 할 것이다. 그로 인해, 당신은 분명히 좋은 구매 결정을 내릴 수 있을 것이다.

구문 해설

4행 The primacy effect is the strong impression {**left** on a consumer by the first information [*that* he or she receives about a certain product]}.
▶ left 이하는 the strong impression을 수식하는 과거분사구
▶ that은 the first information을 선행사로 하는 목적격 관계대명사

15행 ..., they try to promote products ... before there is any chance of *them* **being reviewed** negatively.
▶ being reviewed는 전치사 of의 목적어로 쓰인 동명사구로, 의미상 주어 them(= products)이 '평가되는' 것이므로 수동태로 쓰임

18행 They hope that ... any previous negative opinion [(**that**) a consumer *might have had*].
▶ any previous negative opinion을 선행사로 하는 목적격 관계대명사 that이 생략됨
▶ might have p.p.: ~했을지도 모른다 (과거에 대한 약한 추측)

UNIT 08.
Education

WORD FOCUS　attack

protect 보호하다 / guard 지키다, 보호하다 / secure 안전하게 지키다

WORD CHECK

1. participation　2. constant　3. unite　4. charity
5. achieve
▶ miraculously: in a way that is extraordinary or hard to believe

정답

1. d　2. a　3. The government has started to make efforts to increase the participation of girls in primary schools.　4. c　5. c　6. threat, forbidden, bravery, educational

해석

어느 날, 말랄라 유사프자이라는 이름을 가진 15살의 파키스탄 소녀가 학교에서 집으로 버스를 타고 가고 있었다. 갑자기 탈레반이라는 단체에서 온 한 남자가 버스를 타더니, 그 소녀를 공격하여 그녀는 거의 죽을 뻔했다. 전 세계에 있는 사람들이 충격을 받았고, 왜 어린 소녀가 그런 공격의 표적이 됐는지를 궁금해했다.

파키스탄에 있는 말랄라의 동네는 탈레반 군인들로부터 끊임없이 위협을 받고 있었는데, 그들은 여자아이들이 학교에 가는 것을 금지했다. 말랄라는 BBC 뉴스 블로그에 그런 상황 속에서의 일상이 어떤지를 설명하는 글을 썼다. 또, 그녀는 많은 어린 여자아이들이 학교에 가지 못하는 것이 파키스탄에 얼마나 큰 손해인지에 대해서도 썼다. 탈레반은 이것 때문에 그 소녀에게 몹시 화가 났던 것이다. 기적적으로 말랄라는 공격에서 살아남았다. 그 이후부터 파키스탄의 소녀들을 위해 교육을 개선하고자 계속 맞서 싸우면서 그녀의 목소리는 더욱 강해졌다.

안타깝게도 파키스탄의 여자아이들 중 거의 절반이 학교에 한 번도 가본 적이 없거나 중퇴했다. 적절한 교육과 훈련 없이 이 소녀들은 인생에서 많은 것을 이룰 수 있는 동등한 기회를 절대 갖지 못할 것이다. 하지만 말랄라의 용감한 행동 덕분에 파키스탄 사람들의 태도가 변하고 있다. 이제 그들은 여자아이들에게 있어서 교육의 중요성을 깨닫고 있고, 정부도 여자아이들의 초등 학교 참여를 높이고자 노력을 기울이기 시작했다.

하지만 교육의 부족은 파키스탄의 문제만은 아니다. 전 세계적으로 학교에 가지 못하는 수백만 명의 여자아이들이 있다. 그것이 말랄라가 전 세계의 여자아이들이 교육을 받는 것을 가능하게 하는 것을 목표로 하는 자선 단체인 말랄라 펀드를 시작한 이유이다. 말랄라 펀드는 의식을 고쳐시

키고 전 세계의 여자아이들에게 기회를 제공하기 위해 교육자들과 활동가들을 지원한다.

현재, 말랄라의 용기와 열정 덕분에 전 세계에 있는 사람들이 교육의 중요성을 인정하고 있다. 우리는 세계에 있는 모든 아이들이 마땅히 누려야 할 교육을 받을 수 있도록 말랄라의 선례를 따라 단결해야 한다.

구문 해설

8행 ... from Taliban soldiers, **who** had *forbidden* girls *from going* to school.
▶ who는 Taliban soldiers를 선행사로 하는 계속적 용법의 관계대명사
▶ forbid[prevent] + 목적어 + from v-ing: ~가 …하는 것을 금지하다[막다]

10행 She had also written about {**what** a great loss *it* was **for Pakistan** to have so many young girls [not attending school]}.
▶ what이 이끄는 절은 전치사 about의 목적어로 쓰인 감탄문으로「what + a(n) + 형용사 + 명사 + 주어 + 동사」의 어순
▶ it은 가주어, to have 이하는 진주어이며 for Pakistan은 to부정사의 의미상의 주어

23행 ..., a charity [**whose** goal is to make *it* possible **for girls** all over the world *to access* education].
▶ whose는 a charity를 선행사로 하는 소유격 관계대명사
▶ it은 가목적어, to access 이하는 진목적어이며 for girls는 to부정사의 의미상의 주어

READING 2
p. 44~45

WORD FOCUS economy

global economy 지구촌 경제 / local economy 지역 경제 /
world economy 세계 경제 / market economy 시장 경제

WORD CHECK

1. largely   2. trade   3. vocational   4. evaluate
5. technician
▶ competitive: involving a struggle to win

정답

1. d   2. They are evaluated based upon their school records and natural abilities.   3. a   4. d   5. (1) ⓑ
(2) ⓐ (3) ⓓ (4) ⓒ (5) ⓔ

해석

오늘 저녁 14살의 볼프강은 그의 장비를 준비하고 있다. 내일은 그가 컴퓨터 회사에서 훈련을 받는 첫날이다. 앞으로 3주 동안 볼프강은 자신이 다니고 있는 직업 고등학교 수업을 듣지 않는다. 대신 그는 마이스터

(meister), 즉 '전문적인' 컴퓨터 기술자가 되는 데 도움이 될 업무 경험을 얻게 된다. 10살 된 그의 여동생 안나는 옆방에서 공부하느라 바쁘다. 그녀는 오빠와 다른 학교에 다닌다. 그녀가 다니는 학교에서는 모든 학생들이 나중에 대학에 갈 계획이다.

볼프강과 안나는 독일에 살고 있다. 그곳에서는 아동이 초등학교에 입학하면 같은 학생들과 같은 선생님 밑에서 4년간 같이 지낸다. 4학년 말이 되면 학생들은 학교 성적과 타고난 재능을 토대로 평가를 받는다. 그 후 그들은 대학을 준비하는 인문 학교나 직업 교육을 받는 직업 학교에 들어갈 수 있다.

이러한 교육 제도는 아시아 국가들과 상당히 다르다. 예를 들어 일본의 학생들은 학창 시절 내내 경쟁적인 시험을 치른다. 이 시험이 그들이 어떤 중학교, 고등학교, 대학교에 입학할 수 있는지를 결정한다. 반면에 독일 학생들의 미래는 대체로 초등학교 4학년을 마칠 때쯤이면 결정된다.

독일 학생들은 이 제도에 만족해하는 것 같다. 많은 학생들이 경쟁적인 시험이 적으면 스트레스가 더 적은 환경이 된다고 느낀다. "전 역사나 생물 같은 다른 과목들보다 컴퓨터같이 제가 좋아하는 분야에 집중하고 싶어요." 라고 볼프강은 말한다. 그가 고등학교를 졸업하기 전에 회사에서 얻게 될 업무 경험은 그로 하여금 미래에 좋은 직업을 얻을 수 있게 해 줄 것이다.

독일의 교육 제도는 개인과 국가 모두에게 유익하다. 학생들은 자신만의 특별한 흥미와 재능에 집중할 수 있다. 졸업 후, 그들은 이러한 기술들을 돈을 벌 수 있는 여러 방면에 적용하는 동시에 나라 경제를 더욱 튼튼하게 만들 수 있게 된다.

구문 해설

1행 Tonight, 14-year-old Wolfgang is **getting** his tools **ready**.
▶ get + 목적어 + 형용사: ~를 …하게 하다

12행 They can then attend **either** an academic school to prepare for university **or** a vocational school ....
▶ either A or B: A와 B 둘 중 하나

14행 This system of education **is** quite **different from** *those* of Asian countries.
▶ be different from: ~와 다르다
▶ those: systems of education

17행 ..., students' futures are largely decided **by the time** they finish ....
▶ by the time: ~할 때쯤에

WORD REVIEW TEST

1. b   2. d   3. b   4. c   5. c   6. d   7. b   8. a
9. opposite   10. stuck   11. erase   12. promoted
13. flaw   14. hypothesis   15. commercial
16. tactic

1. a 2. d 3. a 4. d 5. d 6. b 7. a 8. c
9. deserve   10. determined   11. technician
12. opportunity   13. passion   14. attitude
15. apply   16. master

UNIT 09.
Environment

READING 1 p. 48~49

WORD FOCUS impact

major impact 주요한 영향 / social impact 사회적 영향 /
direct impact 직접적인 영향 / negative impact 부정적인 영향

WORD CHECK

1. transport   2. absorb   3. minimal   4. harvest
5. layer
▶ peel: to remove the outer layer of sth

정답

1. b   2. c   3. b   4. The factories burn cork dust to
create up to 90% of the energy they use.   5. a
6. harvested, peeled, regrowing, dust

해석

사람들은 '코르크'라는 단어를 들으면, 보통 와인을 생각한다. 이것은 코르크의 70%가 병마개를 만드는 데 사용되기 때문이다. 하지만 코르크는 악기와 바닥 타일을 포함하여 많은 것을 만드는 데 사용될 수 있다. 게다가 코르크를 사용하는 것은 환경에 최소한의 영향을 끼친다.

코르크나무는 스페인, 이탈리아, 알제리와 같은 여러 지중해 국가에서 재배된다. 세계 제1의 코르크 생산지인 포르투갈은 엄격하게 코르크의 수확을 규제한다. 코르크나무는 적어도 25년 산이 될 때까지는 수확할 수 없다. 그 이후에도 수확은 오직 9년에 한 번씩 이루어진다.

수확할 때는 코르크나무를 베지 않는다. 대신 나무껍질의 바깥층을 벗겨낸다. 이 작업은 나무를 죽이지 않는다. 사실, 나무는 170년 이상 더 살 수 있게 된다. 이 방법에는 또 다른 이점이 있다. 나무가 껍질을 재생시킬 때, 평상시보다 5배 더 많은 이산화탄소를 흡수한다. 이산화탄소는 지구의 온도를 높이는 온실가스 중 하나이다. 따라서 대기로부터 그것을 제거하는 것은 기후 변화를 늦추도록 도와줄 수 있다.

코르크는 수확된 후, 공장으로 옮겨진다. 그곳에서 건조되고, 끓여진 뒤 다양한 제품으로 변하게 된다. 이러한 코르크 공장들 또한 환경친화적이다. 코르크 제품을 생산하는 것은 많은 양의 코르크 가루를 남긴다. 공장에서는 이 가루를 태워 그들이 사용하는 에너지의 90%까지 만들어낸다.

나무에서 벗겨낸 코르크의 거의 모든 것이 버려지지 않는다. 병마개를 만드는 데 사용되는 코르크는 운동용 공에서 엔진 부품까지 다양한 제품으로 재활용될 수도 있다. 그러므로 코르크나무를 재배하는 것이 우리의 행성(지구)을 보호하는 데 도움이 된다고 말할 수 있다. 이러한 이유들로 많은 사람들이 코르크를 거의 완벽한 물질로 여긴다.

구문 해설

(6행) Cork trees can**not** be harvested **until** they are at least 25 years old.
▶ not ~ until ...: …해야 비로소 ~하다

(12행) ..., they absorb **five times more** carbon dioxide **than** they usually *do*.
▶ 배수사 + 비교급 + than ~: ~보다 …배 ~한 (= 배수사 + as + 원급 + as ~)
▶ do는 반복을 피하기 위해 동사 absorb를 대신해 쓰인 대동사

READING 2 p. 50~51

WORD FOCUS convenient

impractical 비실용적인 / uncomfortable 불편한 / awkward 불편한, 다루기 힘든

WORD CHECK

1. triple   2. emission   3. split   4. consumption
5. strict
▶ innovative: new and creative

정답

1. c   2. a   3. They can exchange bags of trash for useful items, such as bus tickets and food.   4. d   5. c
6. development, public, exchange, recycling, traffic

해석

"도시는 문제가 아니다. 그것은 해결책이다." 이 문장은 쿠리치바라는 이름의 브라질 도시의 전 시장인 자이메 레르네르가 한 말이다. 1950년대 이후로 쿠리치바는 도시 계획의 본보기 도시가 되고 있는데, 도시 계획은 도시를 더 편리하고 실용적으로 만들어 주는 도시 설계의 과학이다. 레르네르가 1970년대에 시장이 됐을 때, 그는 이 개념에서 더 나아가 환경친화적인 조치를 취하면서 쿠리치바를 녹색 도시로 만들었다.

쿠리치바의 가장 인상적인 특징 중 하나는 대규모의 녹지 공간이다. 지난 20년간 도시 인구가 세 배로 증가했다는 사실에도 불구하고, 인공의 공원과 숲을 포함하여 1,000개가 넘는 공공녹지 공간이 있다. 이것은 이 도시에 지역 식물들을 개발로부터 보호하는 엄격한 법이 있기 때문이다.

하지만 아마도 쿠리치바의 가장 효과적인 프로젝트는 1991년에 도입된 녹색 교환 프로그램이다. 이 프로그램에서 저소득층 가정은 쓰레기가 든 봉투를 버스표, 음식과 같이 유용한 물건으로 바꿀 수 있다. 아이들이 재활용할 수 있는 제품을 가져오면 그들은 보상으로 학용품, 초콜릿, 장난감

을 받게 된다. 이 프로그램 및 그 밖의 유사 프로그램 때문에 도시 쓰레기의 약 70%가 재활용되고 있고, 이것은 매립지에 끼치는 영향을 줄이고 거리를 깨끗하게 유지한다.

　　마지막으로 쿠리치바의 버스 체계는 도시를 더 살기 좋은 곳으로 만드는 데 큰 역할을 하고 있다. 버스 중 일부는 기차처럼 길고 세 부분으로 나뉜다. 이것은 각 차량이 더 많은 사람들을 수용할 수 있게 해주는데, 이는 교통량과 탄소 배출량 모두를 줄인다. 게다가 얼마나 멀리 이동하든지 간에 버스표 값은 동일하다. 이것은 더 많은 승객을 유치해서 도로의 개인 차량의 수를 크게 줄이고, 그렇게 함으로써 연료 소비를 줄이고 있다.

　　쿠리치바는 종종 지구상에서 가장 지속 가능한 도시 중 하나로 불리는데, 이 타이틀은 단지 운으로 얻은 것이 아니다. 그것은 쿠리치바 시민의 노고와 협력과 더불어 도시 정부의 신중한 계획과 획기적인 프로그램을 통해 얻어진 것이다.

구문 해설

3행　..., Curitiba has been a model city for urban planning, **which** is the science of designing cities ....
▶ which는 urban planning을 선행사로 하는 계속적 용법의 관계대명사 (= and it)

8행　Despite the fact **that** the city's population has tripled in the past 20 years, there are ....
▶ that ... 20 years는 the fact와 동격 관계

23행　This attracts more riders, greatly
┌ **reducing** the number of ...
│ and thereby
└ **lowering** fuel consumption.
▶ reducing과 lowering은 부대상황을 나타내는 분사구문으로, 이 둘은 병렬관계임
▶ the number of: ~의 수

UNIT 10.
Geology

READING 1
p. 52~53

WORD FOCUS threat

great threat 큰 위협 / constant threat 지속적인 위협 / pose a threat 위협을 하다 / receive a threat 위협을 받다

WORD CHECK

1. destroy　2. method　3. lava　4. slope　5. erupt
▶ disaster: a misfortunate or natural event that brings damage

정답

1. c　2. Because the gas bubbles in magma are unable to escape, so pressure builds up over time.　3. d　4. a
5. thin, explosive, slopes, observing, distance

해석

　　화산이 폭발하는 것을 보는 것은 멋지지만 그것은 또한 매우 위험할 수 있다. 홍수나 지진 같은 다른 자연재해들로 해마다 훨씬 더 많은 사람이 사망하지만, 화산은 여전히 세계 많은 지역에서 심각한 위협이다.

　　기본적으로 두 가지 종류의 화산 폭발이 있다. 둘의 결정적인 차이점은 마그마가 얼마나 끈적거리느냐이다. 마그마가 물처럼 묽으면, 가스가 새어 나오기 쉽다. 따라서 폭발성 분출이 일어날 가능성이 거의 없다. 이것은 하와이의 경우에 해당한다. 뜨거운 용암이 가끔 하와이의 유명한 화산들의 가장자리로 흘러넘치지만, 큰 해를 끼치는 경우가 거의 없고 예측하기도 쉽다.

　　반면에 어떤 화산들은 매우 걸쭉한 마그마를 담고 있다. 마그마 내부에서 형성된 가스 거품이 새어 나올 수 없어, 시간이 지나면서 압력이 상승한다. 결국, 마그마가 격렬한 분출로 폭발한다. 이러한 화산 폭발은 매우 위험하고 예측하기 어렵다. 대부분의 유명한 화산 폭발, 예를 들어 고대 폼페이를 멸망시킨 것과 1980년에 세인트헬렌스 산에서 발생한 것이 이 종류였다.

　　그러나 최근에 과학자들은 화산 폭발이 언제 발생할 것이고 얼마나 강력할지를 예측하는 다양한 방법을 실험해오고 있다. 가장 믿을 만한 방법 중 하나는 화산의 흔들림을 측정하는 것이다. 마그마는 지면 깊은 곳으로부터 위로 이동할 때, 수천 번의 작은 지진을 유발한다. 이 지진들의 수가 증가할 때 과학자들은 화산 폭발이 가까워져 오고 있음을 알게 된다. 다른 방법들도 있는데, 화산에서 나오는 가스를 분석하는 것, 화산의 경사면 각도를 측정하는 것, 나아가 그 지역에 사는 동물들의 행동을 관찰하는 것 등이 있다.

　　화산 폭발을 예측하는 것은 중요한 작업이지만, 또한 극도로 위험할 수 있다. 1993년에 10명의 과학자가 그들이 조사하던 콜롬비아 화산이 예기치 않게 폭발하면서 사망했다. 그러한 비극을 막기 위해서, 폭발을 예측하기 위해 취해지는 대부분의 활동은 현재 안전한 거리에서 이루어진다. 폭발이 언제 일어날지 정확히 예측하는 것은 여전히 어렵지만, 과학자들은 계속된 연구로 언젠가 이를 가능하게 만들 것을 희망한다.

구문 해설

8행　Therefore, an explosive eruption **is unlikely to occur.**
▶ be unlikely to-v: ~할 가능성이 거의 없다

11행　The gas bubbles [that form within it] **are unable to escape,** ....
(= magma)
▶ be unable to-v: ~할 수 없다

24행　... were killed in 1993 **when** a Colombian volcano [(that[which]) they were investigating] erupted ....
▶ when은 1993을 선행사로 하는 관계부사

정답

1. ⓑ　2. ⓒ　3. ⓑ　4. the second square　5. ⓒ
6. ⓑ, ⓒ, ⓕ

해석

달 표본 14321

1971년에 나사의 아폴로 14호는 달 표면에 착륙했다. 사진을 찍고 약간의 조사를 한 뒤에, 우주 비행사들은 지구로 가지고 돌아올 월석을 수집했다.

이 암석들 중 하나가 현재 많은 주목을 받고 있다. 그것은 크기가 농구공쯤 되는 9킬로그램의 암석이며, 공식적으로 표본 14321로 알려져 있다. 이 암석은 약 40억 년 전 지구에서 형성되었을지도 모른다. 만약 그렇다면 그것은 이제껏 발견된 것 중 가장 오래된 지구의 암석이 된다.

그 암석은 하나로 합쳐진 많은 작은 조각들로 구성된다. 그중 대부분은 어두우며, 전형적인 달의 물질로 보인다. 그러나, 한 조각은 나머지 다른 것들보다 더 밝고 달보다 지구에서 더 흔하게 발견되는 광물인 지르콘을 포함하고 있다. 과학자들은 지르콘의 화학성분을 분석했고, 표본 14321에서 발견된 한 조각이 강한 압력을 받은 비교적 시원하며 산소가 풍부한 마그마에서 형성되었다고 결론지었다. 이러한 환경은 달에서는 극히 드물다. 그것은 대략 40억 년 전에 지구 표면의 약 20킬로미터 아래서 형성되었을 가능성이 더 크다. 그 당시 지구의 환경은 그 조각이 형성되었을 것으로 여겨지는 환경과 근접하게 맞아떨어졌을 것이다.

그러나 그것이 어떻게 달로 가게 되었을까? 수십 억 년 전 지구는 지속적으로 소행성과 운석에 부딪히고 있었다. 시간이 흐르며 이러한 충돌들은 그 암석을 지구 표면에 점점 더 가까이 오도록 했을지도 모른다. 마침내, 엄청난 충돌이 그것이 달과 부딪쳐 파묻힐 때까지 그것을 우주로 날려 보냈을 수도 있다. 이 추정은 달이 지금보다 지구에 세 배 더 가까웠기 때문에 설득력이 있다. 이후에 또 다른 충돌이 그것을 달 표면 위에 오도록 했을지도 모르는데, 그곳에서 우주 비행사가 그것을 집어 들 때까지 남아 있던 것이다.

표본 14321은 과학자들에게 초창기 지구의 지질학적 환경에 관한 중요한 정보를 제공해 줄지도 모른다. 또한, 달 표면에는 화성과 금성 같은 다른 행성에서 온 암석들이 있을 가능성도 있다. 이것들 또한 과학자들에게 초창기 태양계에 관한 귀중한 자료를 제공해 줄 가능성이 있다.

구문 해설

[5행] This rock **may have formed** on Earth about 4 billion years ago.
▶ may have p.p.: ~했을지도 모른다

[11행] ... in relatively cool, oxygen-rich magma [**that** *had been subjected* to high pressure].
▶ that은 relatively cool, oxygen-rich magma를 선행사로 하는 주격 관계대명사
▶ had been p.p.: 과거완료 수동태 (특정 과거 시점 이전에 일어난 일을 나타냄)
▶ be subjected to: ~을 받다[당하다]

[13행] ..., Earth's conditions would have closely matched the **ones** *in which* the piece is thought *to have formed*.
▶ ones는 앞에 언급된 명사를 대신하는 부정대명사 (= conditions)
▶ in which는 the ones를 선행사로 하며, 관계부사 where로 바꿔 쓸 수 있음
▶ to have p.p.: 언급하는 시점 이전의 일을 나타내는 완료부정사

WORD REVIEW TEST

UNIT 09　　　　　　　　　　　　p. 56

1. d　2. b　3. b　4. c　5. a　6. a　7. c　8. d
9. source　10. affection　11. distribute　12. 1
13. 3

UNIT 10　　　　　　　　　　　　p. 57

1. d　2. b　3. c　4. d　5. d　6. c　7. a　8. b
9. plausible　10. erupted　11. observed　12. sticky
13. assumption　14. surface　15. escape
16. earthquake

UNIT 11.
Culture

READING 1　　　　　　　　　　p. 58~59

WORD FOCUS　aggressive

mild 유순한, 부드러운 / meek 온순한 / gentle 온화한, 순한

WORD CHECK

1. preserve　2. ritual　3. nomadic　4. proverb
5. minority
▶ annual: occurring every year or once a year

정답

1. d　2. ⓒ　3. d　4. c　5. Because overgrazing has reduced local wildlife populations.　6. (1) ⓒ　(2) ⓓ
(3) ⓑ　(4) ⓔ　(5) ⓐ

해석

날개폭이 2미터이고 시속 300킬로미터가 넘는 속도로 날 수 있는 독수리를 상상해 보아라. 이제 그 독수리와 함께 사냥하는 것을 상상해 보아라. 이것은 몽골에서 가장 큰 소수민족인 카자흐족이 수 세기 동안 해온 일이다. 검독수리로 사냥을 하는 것은 그들에게 하나의 삶의 방식이다.

그것은 검독수리들을 포획해 훈련시키는 중요한 의식으로 시작한다. 그 새들은 아직 새끼일 때 포획되고, 암컷들이 더 크고 공격적이기 때문에 수컷보다 선호된다. 훈련의 일환으로 독수리들의 머리 위에 가리개를 씌우고 독수리 주인은 독수리들에게 몇 시간 동안 노래를 불러준다. 이것은 그 새들이 주인의 목소리를 인식하는 것을 배우는 데 도움이 된다. 검독수리는 40년까지 살 수 있지만, 약 10년 동안만 사냥꾼들에게 길러진다. 그 후에는 다시 야생으로 돌려보내 진다.

카자흐족은 섭씨 영하 40도까지 떨어지는 기온에도 불구하고 보통 겨울에 사냥한다. 흰 눈은 독수리들이 토끼와 여우 같은 사냥감을 발견하기 더 쉽게 해준다. 카자흐족의 겨울옷의 중요한 재료인 이 동물들의 털은 연중 이 시기에 가장 두껍기도 하다. 털 외에도, 독수리 사냥은 유목 생활을 하는 카자흐족에게 전통적으로 고기를 제공했다. 과거에 이 (사냥) 기술은 아버지로부터 아들에게 전해졌다. 그러나 오늘날에는 일부 젊은 카자흐족 여성들도 그것을 배운다.

카자흐족 문화를 다음 세대와 전 세계에 홍보하기 위해 1999년 이후로 검독수리 축제가 개최되어 왔다. 약 100명의 사냥꾼이 매년 참가하는 이 축제는 카자흐족의 가장 큰 연례 모임 중 하나다. 행진 후에 사냥꾼들이 그들의 독수리의 기술을 뽐내는 경합이 이어진다. 더 중요한 것은 그 축제가 카자흐족 자긍심의 상징이며 그들의 전통을 보존하도록 돕는다는 점이다.

안타깝게도, 지나친 방목으로 인해 지역의 야생 동물의 개체 수가 줄어들었는데, 이는 사냥감이 훨씬 적어졌다는 것을 의미한다. 게다가, 많은 젊은 카자흐족들이 생계를 유지하기 위해 도시로 이주하고 있다. 그러나, 카자흐족은 결코 그들의 전통적인 생활 방식이 없어지도록 두지는 않을 것 같다. 오래된 카자흐족 속담이 설명하듯, '빠른 말과 맹렬한 독수리는 카자흐족 사람들의 날개다.'

구문 해설

(2행) This is **what** the Kazakhs, the largest minority in
   S V   C
Mongolia, *have been doing* for centuries.

▶ what은 선행사를 포함한 관계대명사

▶ have been v-ing: 현재완료 진행형 (과거부터 현재까지 계속되고 있는 일을 나타냄)

(22행) Sadly, overgrazing has reduced local wildlife
populations, **meaning** there is far less prey *to hunt*.

▶ meaning 이하는 앞 절을 부연 설명하는 분사구문

▶ to hunt는 prey를 수식하는 형용사적 용법의 to부정사

READING 2

p. 60~61

WORD FOCUS   critical

crucial 중대한, 결정적인 / vital 매우 중대한 / significant 중요한 / integral 없어서는 안 될, 필수적인

WORD CHECK

1. empty   2. temporary   3. socialize   4. concern
5. revive
▶ warrior: a brave and experienced soldier

정답

1. b   2. It was banned due to security problems in the region.   3. c   4. c   5. (1) T (2) F   6. a, c

해석

아프리카 북부에 걸쳐 삼백만 제곱마일 넘게 펼쳐진 사하라 사막은 황량하고 텅 빈 곳처럼 보일지도 모른다. 그러나 모로코 남서부 지역의 한 마을인 탄탄에서는 그 사막에 활기를 띠게 해주는 큰 모임이 있다. 매년 5월이나 6월에 30개가 넘는 유목 민족의 수천 명이 탄탄 무셈이라고 불리는 이 행사에 참가한다.

탄탄 무셈은 서로 다른 부족들이 교류하고 그들의 지역 전통을 공유하는 하나의 방식으로서 1963년에 처음 개최되었다. 그 모임은 1970년대 중반에 그 지역의 안보 문제로 인해 한동안 금지되었다. 그러나 2004년에 그 행사를 되살리려는 노력 덕분에 그것은 다시 한번 북아프리카 유목 민족의 가장 큰 모임이 되었다.

축제 기간 동안, 유목 민족들을 수용하기 위해 사막에 수백 개의 텐트들이 세워지면서 일시적인 도시로 바뀌게 된다. 유목 민족들의 전통적인 생활방식의 측면들이 일부 텐트에 전시되는데, 전통 음식과 수제 공예품들이 해당한다. 탄탄 무셈은 또한 낙타 거래와 음악 공연을 비롯한 다양한 행사들이 특징이다. 그러나 이 축제에서 가장 흥미진진한 행사는 Tbourida이다. 이 신나는 공연에서 유목민 전사들이 소총을 공중에 들고 무시무시한 함성을 외치며 말을 탄다.

최근 경제 변화와 기술 발전은 사하라의 유목민 인구가 그들의 전통적인 생활 방식을 유지하는 것을 어렵게 만들었다. 이것은 그들의 문화유산들이 사라질지도 모른다는 우려를 불러일으켰다. 이런 이유로, 탄탄 무셈은 이 부족들의 독특한 전통이 잊히지 않도록 보장하는 데 중요한 역할을 한다.

유네스코는 인류 무형 문화유산에 탄탄 무셈을 등재함으로써 그것의 중요성을 인정했다. 이 특별한 모임은 이제 사하라의 유목 민족들이 그들의 문화를 미래 세대에 전승하도록 돕는 행사로서 세계적으로 인정받는다.

구문 해설

(5행) ..., there is a great gathering [**where** the desert *comes to life*].

▶ where는 a great gathering을 선행사로 하는 관계부사

▶ come to life: 활기를 띠다

9행　... as a way *for different tribes* **to socialize** and **(to)** share their local traditions.

▶ to socialize와 (to) share는 a way를 수식하는 형용사적 용법의 to부정사, for different tribes는 to부정사의 의미상의 주어

19행　..., nomadic warriors ride their horses **while** holding rifles in the air and shouting terrifying war cries.

▶ while 이하는 접속사가 생략되지 않은 분사구문 (= while they hold ....)

23행　..., the Tan-Tan Moussem **plays a** critical **role in** *ensuring* [**that** these tribes' unique traditions are not forgotten].

▶ play a role in: ~에서 역할을 하다

▶ ensuring 이하는 전치사 in의 목적어로 쓰인 동명사구

▶ that 이하는 ensuring의 목적어 역할

UNIT 12.
Music

READING 1　　　　　　　　　　　　　　　p. 62~63

WORD FOCUS　frequent

repeated 되풀이되는 / recurring 반복되어 발생되는 /
continual 빈번한, 거듭되는

WORD CHECK

1. scrawl　2. note　3. manuscript　4. substitution
5. handy

▶ legend: a story about famous people or events in the past

정답

1. d　2. d　3. It was scrawled messily across several pages, with frequent scratch-outs and substitutions.
4. d　5. sheet, sounded, tuned, talented

해석

　　음악에서 초견(연주)은 전에 한 번도 보거나 들은 적이 없는 곡을 단지 악보를 읽어 연주하는 것을 말한다. 대부분의 음악가들이 유창하게 이것을 하려고 고군분투하는 반면, 과거의 유명한 작곡가들의 놀라운 초견 능력에 대한 전설적인 이야기가 있다. 이 천재들은 마치 몇 년 동안 연주해온 것처럼 음악을 즉석에서 연주할 수 있었다.

볼프강 아마데우스 모차르트도 그러한 천재 중 한 명이었다. 어떤 연습이나 시연 없이도, 그는 악보를 보고 마지막 한 음까지 완벽하게 피아노로 연주할 수 있었다. 이런 능력은 직접 곡을 쓸 때 그에게 도움이 되었는데, 그는 곡의 각 음을 적거나 연주해보기 전에 어떤 소리가 될지를 항상 알고 있었기 때문이다.

루트비히 판 베토벤도 비슷한 능력이 있었는데, 한번은 음이 맞지 않는 피아노 때문에 한 협주곡 전체를 새로운 키로 연주했던 것으로 유명하다. 이것은 마치 배우에게 공연 시작 5분 전에 영어 대신 스웨덴어로 대사하라고 요구하는 것과 마찬가지이다. 모차르트와 마찬가지로, 베토벤은 음을 연주하지 않고도 머리로 그것을 '들을' 수 있었고, 이것은 그가 완전히 귀를 먹었음에도 불구하고 작곡을 계속해 나갔던 인생 후반에 중요한 역할을 했다.

그러나 대부분의 학자는 프란츠 리스트가 초견(연주)에 가장 재능이 있었을 것이라는 데 동의한다. 학생 작곡가 한 명이 리스트에게 자신이 방금 쓴 피아노 협주곡을 가져온 일화가 있다. 그 곡은 몇 페이지에 걸쳐 지저분하게 휘갈겨 쓴 것으로, 여러 번 줄을 그어 지우고 다시 써넣은 흔적이 있었다. 하지만, 리스트는 학생에게서 원고를 받아 잠깐 훑어보고, 오케스트라 파트까지 포함하여 전체 악보를 음 하나 놓치지 않고 계속해서 연주했다! 그의 솜씨는 매우 뛰어나서 역사상 알려진 모든 곡을 완벽하게 연주했다고 전해진다.

구문 해설

14행　... and is famous for once **having played** an entire concerto in a new key due to an out-of-tune piano.

▶ having played는 언급하는 시점 이전에 있었던 일을 나타내는 완료동명사로 전치사 for의 목적어 역할

17행　..., Beethoven could mentally "hear" notes **without playing** them, *which* became important later in his life ....

▶ without v-ing: ~하지 않고

▶ which는 앞 절 전체를 선행사로 하는 계속적 용법의 관계대명사

25행　His skill was **so** great **that** he is said *to have given* a perfect performance ....

▶ so ~ that ...: 너무 ~하여 …하다

▶ to have p.p.: 언급하는 시점 이전의 일을 나타내는 완료부정사

READING 2　　　　　　　　　　　　　　　p. 64~65

WORD FOCUS　fortune

a huge fortune 막대한 재산 / leave a fortune 재산을 남기다 /
inherit a fortune 재산을 상속받다

WORD CHECK

1. elegant　2. console　3. revival　4. enthusiast
5. immigrant

▶ melancholic: feeling sad or depressed

1. d   2. c   3. He introduced tango through radio and the movies, which made it a worldwide phenomenon. 4. ⓐ   5. ⓑ-ⓔ-ⓓ   6. a, d

해석

오늘날, 사람들이 '탱고'라는 단어를 들으면 그들은 보통 대중적이고 활기찬 스타일의 춤을 떠올린다. 그러나 원래 그것은 슬픈 사람들과 외로운 사람들을 위로하기 위해 사용된 음악의 한 형식을 가리켰다.

1880년대에 유럽에서 무일푼인 수천 명의 이민자가 부자가 되기를 바라며 아르헨티나의 대평원으로 건너왔다. 그러나 많은 사람들이 실패했고 부에노스아이레스의 빈민가로 모여들었다. 이 이민자들은 상실감과 외로움을 느꼈고 음악을 통해 자신들의 불행을 나누었다. 그들은 아프리카 노예의 리듬과 스페인 식민지 이주민들의 소리를 이용해 자신들만의 독특한 음악과 춤을 만들어냈다. 이 음악에 깃든 슬픈 정서는 아코디언의 일종인 반도네온의 구슬픈 소리에 의해 두드러졌다. 이때 이후로, 탱고가 발달하기 시작했다.

1차 세계대전이 끝난 후, 탱고는 아르헨티나의 지배적인 음악 스타일이 되었다. 아르헨티나의 경제가 점차 발전함에 따라 탱고를 더 세련되고 우아하게 만들기 위해 그것은 다듬어졌다. 노랫말은 가난과 이민자의 외로움이라는 주제에서 사랑이라는 보편적인 주제로 차츰 옮겨 갔다. 가수나 무용수, 작사가, 작곡가 등의 스타도 탄생했다. 유명 가수인 카를로스 가르델은 탱고를 라디오와 영화를 통해 소개했는데, 이는 그 음악을 세계적인 현상으로 만들었다.

그러나 1930년 아르헨티나에서는 무력에 의한 정부 교체가 있었다. 사람들은 많은 다른 자유와 함께 투표할 권리를 잃었다. 침울한 분위기가 나라 전역에 퍼졌고, 이는 노래와 춤에 관심을 가지는 사람이 거의 없게 만들었다. 1930년대 후반이 되어서야 아르헨티나 사람들은 자유를 되찾았다. 그들은 탱고를 즐기기 시작했고, 탱고는 다시 한번 그들 일상의 일부가 되었다. 그러나 탱고는 1940년대 이후에는 미국의 스윙과 로큰롤의 유입으로 인해 인기가 떨어졌다. 1960년대에서 1980년대까지, 탱고는 나이든 세대와 소수의 애호가에 의해서만 즐겨졌다.

최근의 부흥은 1980년대 초반부터 시작되는데, 이때 〈탱고 아르헨티나〉라는 무대 공연이 탱고의 매혹적인 형태로 전 세계 순회공연을 했다. 1990년대는 탱고가 재즈와 같은 현대 음악의 영향을 받으면서 또 다른 부흥기가 되었다.

구문 해설

18행 **It** was *not until* the late 1930s **that** Argentinians got their freedom back.
▶ It ~ that ... 강조구문으로 부사구인 not until the late 1930s를 강조
▶ not until: ~이후에야 비로소

26행 ..., **with** tango **being** influenced by contemporary music like jazz.
▶「with + 명사 + 분사」 구문은 '~가 …한 채로'로 해석하며, 명사와 분사는 주어와 서술어 관계임

WORD REVIEW TEST

UNIT 11   p. 66

1. a   2. d   3. b   4. c   5. c   6. d   7. a   8. b
9. harsh   10. released   11. stretched   12. show off
13. craft   14. prey   15. acknowledge
16. aggressive

UNIT 12   p. 67

1. b   2. c   3. d   4. b   5. a   6. d   7. c   8. d
9. b   10. a   11. c   12. composer   13. rehearsal
14. glance

UNIT 13.
Art

READING 1   p. 68~69

WORD FOCUS   message

clear message 명확한 메시지 / urgent message 속보 / leave a message 메시지를 남기다 / deliver a message 메시지를 전달하다

WORD CHECK

1. functional   2. specific   3. originate   4. stroke
5. fancy
▶ literally: in the strictest definition

정답

1. a   2. It is being able to control the rhythm and movement of your pen strokes when you write.   3. b
4. c   5. b   6. elegant, usual, harmony, please

해석

당신은 예술적 재능이 있고 글씨를 잘 쓰는가? 만약 그렇다면, 캘리그래피를 고려해봐도 좋을 것이다. 문자 그대로는 '아름다운 글'이라는 뜻으로, 이것은 글자나 문자, 단어, 문장을 세련되고 멋진 방법으로 쓰는 예술이다.

전문 캘리그래퍼가 되는 비결은 글씨를 쓸 때 펜 놀림의 리듬과 움직임을 조절할 줄 아는 것이다. 캘리그래피는 다소 까다로운 예술 형태 중 하나인데, 각각의 문자나 글자를 쓸 기회가 한 번밖에 없기 때문이다. 각 작업은 순식간에 즉흥적으로 완성된다. 가장 중요한 점은, 되돌아가 실수를 바로잡을 수 없다는 것이다. 예술가가 일단 쓰는 것을 멈추면, 작업은 끝난다.

하지만, 캘리그래피는 단지 전문적인 기술 그 이상의 것이다. 전문 캘리그래퍼는 자신의 작품에 특유의 정서를 표현할 수 있어야 한다. 그들은 자신이 쓰는 말의 의미뿐만 아니라 그 형태와 모양을 통해서도 이를 구현한다. 캘리그래퍼의 펜 놀림 하나하나는 나머지와 조화를 이루어야, 보는 사람들에게 깊은 느낌을 불러일으킬 수 있는 작품이 된다.

현대 캘리그래피에는 두 가지 본질적인 측면이 있다. <u>한편으로는</u>, 그것은 회화나 조각처럼 순수한 형태의 예술이 될 수 있다. 이러한 유형의 캘리그래피에서는 단어 그 자체는 읽힐 수도, 읽히지 않을 수도 있다. 중요한 것은 바로 그것의 모양이다. 하지만, 캘리그래피는 또한 메시지를 시각적으로 보기 좋게 전달하는 방법으로 사용되기도 한다. 이와 같은 실용적인 캘리그래피는 화려한 결혼식 초청장이나 인사카드에서 가장 흔하게 발견된다. 놀랍게도, 이것은 우리가 이메일을 보낼 때마다 사용되기도 한다. 이메일 주소에 쓰이는 @라는 기호는 수백 년 전의 캘리그래피로부터 비롯된 것이라고 여겨진다.

그러니 캘리그래피에 한번 도전해 보는 게 어떤가? 아름다운 글자나 문자를 서로 조화를 이루게 씀으로써, 당신은 그것을 보는 모든 사람에게 특별한 메시지를 전하는 자신만의 예술작품을 만들어낼 수 있다.

구문 해설

[10행] ..., **there is no going** back and **correcting** errors.
  ▶ there is no v-ing: ~할 수 없다, ~하는 것은 불가능하다
[13행] They do this **not just** through the meaning of the words they write, **but also** through their ....
  ▶ not just[only] A but also B: A뿐만 아니라 B도
[22행] The @ symbol, used in email addresses, **is believed _to have originated_** from calligraphy ....
  ▶ be believed to-v: ~인 것으로 믿어지다[여겨지다]
  ▶ to have p.p.: 언급하는 시점 이전의 일을 나타내는 완료부정사

READING 2   p. 70~71

WORD CHECK

1. unknowable   2. treachery   3. reaction
4. perception   5. rational

▶ plenty: a large amount

정답

1. d   2. His paintings are known for making viewers think about the concept of reality, but doing so with a clever sense of humor.   3. a   4. reality   5. c
6. surrealism, rational, imagination, perception

해석

초현실주의 화가: 르네 마그리트

당신은 그림이 현실을 정확하게 나타내야 한다고 생각하는가? 그렇다면 르네 마그리트의 그림은 당신이 다시 생각하게 할지도 모른다. 마그리트는 흥미로운 초현실주의 이미지를 많이 만들어낸 벨기에의 유명한 미술가였다. 그의 그림은 보는 사람으로 하여금 실체라는 개념에 대해서 생각하게 만드는데, 재치 있는 유머 감각으로 그렇게 하는 것으로 유명하다.

마그리트는 초현실주의 사조의 일원이었는데, 초현실주의는 부분적으로는 제1차 세계대전의 공포에 대한 반발로서 생겨났다. 예술가들은 세계를 전쟁으로 이끈 것은 바로 과도한 합리적 사고라고 여겼다. 마그리트와 다른 초현실주의 작가들은 그보다는 창의력과 상상력을 가지고 자신을 표현하는 데 중점을 두었다.

마그리트는 대개 친숙한 사물들을 그리면서도, 그것들을 평범하지 않은 환경에 배치하여 일상적인 사물에 새로운 의미를 부여했다. 그의 가장 유명한 작품 중 하나인 〈이미지의 배반〉은 아무 무늬가 없는 배경을 바탕으로 한 단순한 파이프의 이미지이다. 그러나 그 아래에, 마그리트는 "Ceci n'est pas une pipe."라는 말을 썼다. 이는 "이것은 파이프가 아니다."라는 뜻의 프랑스어이다. 그는 이렇게 해서 보는 사람으로 하여금 실제 파이프와 파이프 이미지 간의 차이에 대해서 생각하도록 만들었다.

〈청강실〉도 마그리트가 간단한 방식으로 일상적인 사물을 그렸다는 점에서 유사한데, 이 (작품의) 경우에는 사과이다. 그러나 그는 사과가 빈방을 가득 채울 정도로 커다랗게 보이게 함으로써 우리의 인식에 의심을 제기한다. 다시 한번, 보는 사람들은 이미지와 실체 간의 차이에 대해서 생각하게 된다.

한번은 마그리트가 자신의 작품에 대해 질문을 받고 이렇게 말한 적이 있었다. "누군가 내 그림 중 하나를 보면, 스스로에게 '저건 무슨 의미이지?'라는 간단한 질문을 합니다. 그건 아무 의미가 없는데, 미스터리 역시 아무 의미가 없기 때문이죠. 그건 알 수 없는 것입니다." 하지만, 이 그림들의 참된 의미는 알 수 없을지라도, 이 그림들은 미술 애호가들에게 여전히 많은 생각할 거리들을 준다.

구문 해설

[17행] _The Listening Room_ is similar **in that** Magritte painted an everyday object ....
  ▶ in that: ~라는 점에서
[23행] When (**he was**) asked about his artwork, Magritte once said, ...
  ▶ 부사절의 주어가 주절의 주어와 같을 경우 「주어 + be동사」는 종종 생략함
[26행] ..., they still **provide** art lovers **with** <u>plenty to think about</u>.
  ▶ provide A with B: A에게 B를 제공하다

UNIT 14.
Human Rights

READING 1   p. 72~73

WORD FOCUS   correct

fix 고치다 / adjust 조정하다, 바로잡다 / amend 고치다, 개선하다

WORD CHECK

1. property   2. guarantee   3. govern
4. independence   5. demand
▶ injustice: unfair situation or conditions

정답

1. d   2. a   3. It listed the injustices suffered by women in the US and proposed resolutions to correct them.   4. d   5. b   6. (1) ⓓ (2) ⓑ (3) ⓐ (4) ⓒ

해석

　1776년 미국 독립 선언서 작성자들이 "우리는 다음과 같은 사실을 자명한 진리로 받아들인다. 즉 모든 남자는 평등하게 태어났고 …"라고 썼을 때, 그들은 문자 그대로 'men(남자들)'이라는 단어를 사용했다. 여성들은 독립 선언서 및 미국 헌법에 보장되어 있던 권리 중 다수에서 제외되었다. 여성들이 마침내 모든 인간이 받아 마땅한 기본권을 보장받는 데는 144년이 더 걸렸다.

　여권에 대해 논의하기 위한 최초의 회의가 1848년 엘리자베스 캐디 스탠턴과 루크리셔 모트에 의해서 소집되었다. 행사가 열린 뉴욕의 마을 이름을 딴 세네카 폴스 회의에서 스탠턴은 독립 선언서에 기초하여 자신이 직접 쓴 감성선언서를 낭독하였다. 그 선언서에는 미국 내에서의 여성들이 겪는 부당한 일들이 나열되었고 이를 바로잡기 위한 결의안이 제안되었다.

　그녀의 불평등 목록 중 첫 번째는 여성에게 투표권이 허락되어 있지 않다는 사실인데, 이는 곧 여성들이 자신의 삶을 지배하는 법률을 제정하는 데 있어 아무런 의견도 내지 못한다는 뜻이었다. 또한, 기혼여성의 경우 그들의 재산은 전적으로 남편의 소유였다. 여성은 교육도 받을 수 없고, 전문직에 종사할 수도 없었으며, 교회 일에 공식적으로 참여할 수 있는 권리도 없었다.

　선언서에 제시된 결의안은 법률 및 사회의 모든 분야에서 여성을 남성과 동등하게 인정해 달라고 요구했다. 선언서는 여성들이 시민으로서의 자신의 권리를 요구할 것과 남성들이 여성들의 삶과 재산을 지배하도록 하는 관습을 종식시킬 것을 요구했다. 신문 및 종교 지도자들은 세네카 폴스 회의 때 이루어진 행사들을 조롱했고 결의안의 내용을 비난했다. 그럼에도 불구하고 세네카 폴스 회의는 미국 내 여권 신장 운동의 중요한 첫 단계가 되었다. 마침내 1920년에 미국 헌법이 공식적으로 개정되자, 21세가 넘는 여성들에게 투표권이 주어졌다.

구문 해설

7행   **It took** women 144 more years **to finally receive** the basic rights [that all human beings deserve].
▶ It takes + A + 시간 + to-v: A가 ~하는 데 …의 시간이 걸리다

14행   First on her list of injustices was the fact **that** women were not allowed to vote, which meant ....
　　C　　　　　　　　　　　　V　　S └ = ┘
▶ 보어가 강조되어 문장 맨 앞으로 나오면서 주어와 동사가 도치됨
▶ that이 이끄는 절은 the fact와 동격 관계

18행   The resolutions in the declaration **demanded** that women (**should**) **be** recognized as ....
▶ 요구 · 주장을 나타내는 동사(demand)의 목적어인 that절의 동사는 「(should +) 동사원형」으로 씀

READING 2   p. 74~75

WORD FOCUS   enormous

huge 거대한 / massive 대규모의 / immense 엄청난, 막대한

WORD CHECK

1. discuss   2. estimate   3. ongoing   4. network
5. publish
▶ pressure: to try to make sb do sth forcefully

정답

1. d   2. They are the rights to education, protection against exploitation, and relief in all circumstances.
3. d   4. b   5. (1) T (2) F   6. education, participated, awareness, fight

해석

　1959년에 국제 연합은 아동 권리 선언이라고 불리는 아동의 권리 목록에 동의했다. 그 목록에는 교육에 대한 권리, 착취로부터의 보호, 그리고 모든 상황에서의 구조를 포함한 열 개의 조항이 있다. 그러나 이 선언에도 불구하고 많은 아동들이 혹독한 환경에서 일하도록 강요받았기 때문에 이러한 권리들을 누릴 수 없었다.

　거의 40년 후인 1998년에 카일라시 사티아르티라는 이름의 인도 인권 운동가가 계속되는 문제에 대항하는 대규모 시위인 아동 노동에 반대하는 글로벌 행진을 조직했다. 그 당시 전 세계에 아직도 2억 5천만 명의 아동 노동자들이 있는 것으로 추정되었다. 예를 들어 미국에서는 약 23만 명의 아동들이 과일과 채소를 따며 농장에서 불법적으로 일하고 있었고, 그중 약 45퍼센트가 학교를 중퇴했다. 이와 비슷하거나 더 심각한 상황들이 전 세계 국가들에 존재했다.

　아동 노동에 반대하는 글로벌 행진은 1998년 1월 17일에 시작했고 103개국에서 진행되었다. 7백만 명이 넘는 사람들이 변화를 요구하기 위해 그 시위에 참가했다. 일부 참가자들은 그들의 지역 내에서만 행진했고,

다른 이들은 카일라시 사티아르티와 함께 스위스 제네바로 가서 행진을 이어나갔다. 이곳에서는 국제 노동 기구(ILO)가 아동 노동 문제에 대한 해결책을 논의하기 위해 회합하고 있었다. 6월에 사티아르티와 다른 행진 참가자들은 제네바의 국제 연합 사무소로 들어가 ILO와 함께 그 문제를 해결해 줄 것을 강력히 주장했다.

그 행진은 대단한 성공이었는데, 왜냐하면 그것이 (아동 노동) 문제에 대해 관심을 끌어모았고 ILO로 하여금 아동 노동을 규제하는 효과적인 법을 만들도록 압력을 주었기 때문이다. ILO가 도달한 합의는 그들이 발표했던 다른 어떤 근로 기준들보다 더 빠르게 전 세계 국가들에서 받아들여졌다. 그때 이후로 상황은 점차 개선되었으나 그 문제는 지속되고 있다. 아직도 약 1억 5천 2백만 명의 아동 노동자들이 착취당하고 있기 때문에 투쟁은 계속되고 있다. 오늘날, 아동 노동에 반대하는 글로벌 행진은 하나의 행사로서보다는 조직으로서 존재한다. 선생님, 노동조합, 그리고 다른 집단의 연계망으로서, 그것은 아동의 자유와 교육에 대한 권리를 보호하기 위해 나날이 노력한다.

구문 해설

9행 ..., around 230,000 children were illegally working on farms **picking** fruit and vegetables, ...
▶ picking 이하는 동시동작을 나타내는 분사구문

21행 The agreement [(**that**[**which**]) the ILO reached] was accepted by nations around the world *faster than any other set* of labor standards ....
▶ the ILO 앞에 목적격 관계대명사 that[which]이 생략됨
▶ 비교급 + than any other + 단수명사: 다른 어떤 ~보다 더 …한 (최상급의 의미)

WORD REVIEW TEST

UNIT 13
p. 76

1. a 2. b 3. c 4. d 5. b 6. b 7. c 8. a
9. fancy 10. strokes 11. perception
12. unknowable 13. reality 14. plain
15. harmony 16. horror

UNIT 14
p. 77

1. d 2. a 3. c 4. b 5. b 6. c 7. d 8. a
9. takes place 10. activists 11. excluded
12. estimated 13. effective 14. march
15. criticize 16. exploitation

UNIT 15.
Astronomy

READING 1
p. 78~79

WORD FOCUS sign

a clear sign 명확한 징후 / a hopeful sign 희망적인 조짐 / detect signs 징후를 발견하다

WORD CHECK

1. frozen 2. glowing 3. reflect 4. predict
5. astronomer
▶ observe: to watch sth closely

정답

1. c 2. c 3. b 4. It causes some of the frozen dust and gas to melt and burn away. 5. b 6. (1) ⓑ (2) ⓐ (3) ⓑ (4) ⓐ

해석

1835년 11월, 혜성이 하늘을 밝게 비출 때, 한 아기가 태어났다. 그 아기는 자라서 위대한 작가인 마크 트웨인이 되었다. 1909년에 그는 다음과 같이 말했다. "나는 1835년에 혜성과 함께 왔다. 그것은 내년에 또 올 것이며, 나는 그것과 함께 가기를 바란다." 그리고 그는 그렇게 했다! 마크 트웨인은 1910년 그 혜성이 다시 나타난 다음 날 사망했다.

그 혜성은 우리 태양계에서 가장 유명한 천체 중 하나인 핼리 혜성이었다. 천문학자들은 1조 개에 달하는 많은 혜성이 우주를 향해하고 있을 것으로 생각한다. 하지만, 이들 중 불과 수천 개만이 실제로 관측되었다.

사람들은 기원전 240년부터 핼리 혜성을 목격해 왔다. 그것은 하늘을 가로질러 움직이는 빛나는 꼬리를 가진 별처럼 보인다. 아주 오랫동안 많은 사람들은 핼리 혜성이 불운을 상징하는 흉조라고 믿었다. 그러나 1705년에 에드먼드 G. 핼리라는 영국의 한 천문학자가 사람들의 생각을 바꿔 놓았다. 그는 그의 저서에서 1531년, 1607년 그리고 1682년에 목격된 혜성들이 사실은 76년마다 되돌아오는 하나의 혜성이라고 말했다. 그는 또한 그 혜성이 1758년에 다시 올 것이라고 예측했다. 불행히도, 핼리는 그것을 볼 때까지 살지 못했다. 하지만 1758년에 혜성이 나타나자, 그의 이론은 증명되었고, 혜성은 그의 이름을 따서 이름 붙여졌다.

핼리 혜성은 얼어붙은 먼지와 가스로 이루어진 매우 큰 원형체이다. 우리는 그것이 태양계를 가로질러 움직일 때, 대부분의 경우 그것을 보지 못한다. 그러나 76년마다 한 번씩, 그것은 태양과 근접하여 지나는데, 태양의 열은 얼어붙은 먼지와 가스 일부를 녹이거나 태운다. 불타는 먼지와 가스는 태양 빛을 반사해서 핼리 혜성의 유명한 꼬리로 나타나게 된다. 바로 이때가 우리가 핼리 혜성이 밤하늘을 눈부시게 가로질러 움직이는 것을 볼 수 있는 유일한 때이다.

2행 The baby grew up **to be** the great writer Mark Twain.

▶ to be는 결과를 나타내는 부사적 용법의 to부정사

18행 ..., it passes near the Sun, the heat **of which** causes some of the frozen dust and gas to melt ....

▶ of which는 the Sun을 선행사로 하는 소유격 관계대명사

READING 2　TOEFL　　p. 80~81

정답

1. ⓐ　2. ⓓ　3. ⓓ　4. the third square　5. ⓒ
6. ⓐ, ⓓ, ⓕ

해석

토성

　태양으로부터 여섯 번째 행성인 토성은 크고 뚜렷한 고리들로 알려져 있다. 이 고리들은 1610년 갈릴레오 갈릴레이에 의해 처음으로 관측되었지만 아주 명확하게 보인 것은 아니었다. 그는 자신이 그 행성의 두 개의 큰 위성을 보고 있는 것은 아닌지 궁금해했다. 이후에, 더 좋은 망원경을 이용해 천문학자들이 그 고리들의 형태를 식별할 수 있었고, 마침내 그것들이 물질의 수많은 작은 조각들로 이루어졌음을 발견했다.

　1980년대에 두 대의 보이저 우주 탐사선이 토성에 관한 더 상세한 정보를 수집했고, 카시니 탐사선을 이용해 2004년부터 2017년까지 탐사가 계속되었다. 이 우주선에 의해 촬영된 상세한 이미지들 덕분에 우리는 토성이 수많은 작은 고리들로 둘러싸여 있는 것을 알게 되었다. 수집된 정보는 토성의 고리들이 무엇으로 만들어져 있는지, 그것들이 어디에서 왔을지와 그것들이 어떻게 변화하는지에 관한 정보를 밝혀냈다.

　수십억 개의 각 조각들이 토성의 고리를 형성한다. 몇몇은 크기가 산만 하고, 다른 것들은 모래알만 하다. 그것들은 주로 얼어붙은 물로 이루어져 있다. 망원경을 통해 관측될 때, 그 고리들은 하나의 커다란 원반처럼 보인다. 그러나 실제로는 네 개의 주요 고리 집단과 세 개의 더 작은 집단이 있으며, 모두 간극으로 분리되어 있다. 그것들은 모두 빠른 속도로 그 행성(토성)의 궤도를 돈다.

　처음에 천문학자들은 그 고리들이 행성(토성)만큼 오래되었으며 토성이 형성될 때 남겨진 물질들로 만들어졌다고 생각했다. 그러나 그 고리들은 매우 순수한 얼음으로 만들어져 있다는 것이 드러났는데, 이는 그것들이 그 행성보다 훨씬 젊다는 것을 암시한다. 만약 그것들이 오래된 것이라면, 그것들은 먼지를 더 많이 축적했을 것이다. 그 대신, 천문학자들은 이제 그 고리들이 깨어진 위성들로 만들어졌을 수도 있다고 생각한다. 먼 과거에 소행성이나 혜성이 토성의 위성들과 충돌하여 그것들을 산산조각 냈을 가능성이 더 많다. 그 후에 그 조각들이 넓게 퍼져 토성 주위에 고리들을 형성했을 수도 있다.

　고리들이 어떻게 형성되었는지와 관계없이, 과학자들은 행성의 수명에 견주었을 때 고리들이 오래가지 않을 것임에 동의한다. 토성의 자기장이 고리 입자들을 안으로 끌어당겨서 그것들이 그 행성에 비처럼 내리게 한다. 고리들은 점차 질량이 줄어들고 있고 아마도 3억 년 내로 사라질 것이다.

9행 The collected data revealed information about [**what** Saturn's rings are made of], [**where** they *might have come* from] and [**how** they change].

▶ what ... made of, where ... come from, how ... change는 전치사 about의 목적어 역할을 하는 간접의문문으로 「의문사 + 주어 + 동사」의 어순

▶ might have p.p.: ~했을지도 모른다

13행 When (**they are**) seen through a telescope, the rings look like one large disk.

▶ 주절의 주어와 부사절의 주어가 같을 때 부사절의 「주어 + be동사」는 생략할 수 있음

18행 If they **were** old, they **would have collected** more dust.

▶ 종속절이 가정법 과거, 주절이 가정법 과거완료인 혼합 가정법

WORD REVIEW TEST

UNIT 15　　p. 82

1. d　2. a　3. c　4. b　5. b　6. a　7. d　8. c
9. d　10. b　11. a　12. c　13. solar　14. gap
15. comet　16. theory

READING
EXPERT